T5-AWI-744

Private Schools and
State Schools

Private Schools and State Schools:

Two Systems or One?

Daphne Johnson

Open University Press

Milton Keynes · Philadelphia

Open University Press
Open University Educational Enterprises Limited
12 Cofferidge Close
Stony Stratford
Milton Keynes MK11 1BY, England

and
242 Cherry Street
Philadelphia, PA 19106, USA

First Published 1987

British Library Cataloguing in Publication Data
Johnson, Daphne, *1927–*
Private schools and state schools: two
systems or one?
1. Private schools – Great Britain
I. Title
371'.02'0941   LC53.G7

ISBN 0 335 15998 2

ISBN 0 335 15997 4 Pbk

Library of Congress Cataloguing-in-Publication Data
Johnson, Daphne.
Private schools and state schools.
Bibliography: p.
Includes index.
1. Education—Great Britain.   2. Private schools—
Great Britain.   3. Public schools, Endowed (Great Britain)
4. Public schools—Great Britain.   5. School, Choice of—
Great Britain.   I. Title.
LA632.J57   1987   373.2'22'0941   86–43213

ISBN 0–335–15998–2
ISBN 0–335–15997–4 (pbk.)

Text design by Carlton Hill
Typeset by Rowland Phototypesetting Limited
Bury St Edmunds, Suffolk
Printed in Great Britain at
The Alden Press, Oxford

Remembering C.D.J., and
her thirteen years
of Happiest Days.

Contents

Contents

Preface

Should private education and public education in Britain be seen as inter-connected, or are they totally separate, mutually antipathetic, systems?

To provide a new perspective on this long unresolved question of education policy, I have drawn on the experience of providers and users of both forms of education. My exploratory study, carried out in 1984 and 1985, was made possible by a generous grant from the Leverhulme Trust to the Department of Government, Brunel University. Informants have included education officers, local councillors, and headteachers of independent and maintained schools, who are providers of education in an area of the south-east of England. I am glad to acknowledge their help. The users' view of the schools comes from families in the same area who used both private schools and state schools for their children's education. I extend my thanks to all the parents who told me about their experiences, and especially the twenty-five families whose homes I visited.

The coexistence of private and public education in a given geographical area has to be understood in the context of a broader knowledge. I am grateful to representatives of Her Majesty's Inspectorate, the Service Children's Education Authority, the Foreign and Commonwealth Office, the Boarding Schools Association, the Independent Schools Information Service, the Independent Schools Joint Council and the Independent Schools Bursars Association, all of whom were at pains to ensure that I was not lacking in background information.

Irene Fox, Geoff Whitty and John Welton have helped me by discussing their own related research. Colin Fletcher's interest and encouragement made a big difference. John Burnett and Maurice Kogan were also helpful in their comments on sections of my script. My closest colleague throughout the work has been Valerie Trott, whose contribution as project secretary has been well beyond the call of duty, sustaining me in some times of difficulty.

xi

My many helpers are not accountable for the judgments made or the viewpoints included in or omitted from my book. For these I take full responsibility.

Terminology

The vocabulary of public and private education is extensive and somewhat confusing. 'State education' and 'state schools' are colloquial terms, useful for making general reference to schools of the public sector. It is, however, more correct to refer to 'local authority', or 'maintained' schools, for in Britain public education is locally administered, and schools in the public sector are maintained by local education authorities.

Voluntary-aided and voluntary-controlled schools are also part of public education, being largely maintained by the local education authority, with only a small proportion of costs being met by the foundation (usually religious) which established them.

In describing private education, the main impediment to clarity is the term 'public schools'. These are a group of long established *private* schools. 'Private education' or 'the private sector' comprises all schools at which fees are charged for some pupils. The term 'public schools' is inappropriate for schools at which fees are charged. Except when quoting the words of others, I refer to them as 'famous' schools. 'Independent schools' is another term used for schools in the private sector, and is the one most frequently employed here.

This whole book is about the existence alongside one another of two sectors of education: public and private. As a shorthand term for this state of affairs I use the expression 'educational coexistence'.

Daphne Johnson
Brunel University

Introduction

If he doesn't get on well at the ordinary school, we might try the private.

Mother of pre-school child

We really have no idea, from year to year, what will be the pressure for places in our sixth form colleges. It depends how many sixteen year olds decide they want to move over from the private sector.

Education officer

These two remarks give an indication of the main task of this book: to explore what it means, both for the users and the providers of education, that private schools and state schools exist side by side.

The parent who thought she might make use of private education had no previous experience of it. But because private schools exist, and because the maintained sector of education is not without its problems, many ordinary families wonder if a private school might suit one child if not all children in the family. They wonder if such a school might be preferable for one stage of education if not for all stages. It is no longer adequate to assume that children in private schools come from a distinct social stratum, a group ideologically and socially committed to the notion of independent schooling. In later chapters the experience of twenty-five families who have used *both* sectors of education for their children is explored in depth.

The education officer's comment about a possible influx of pupils from the private sector shows the significance of the coexistence of public and private education from a provider's point of view. In this country two groups provide education: the local education authorities, with their maintained schools and colleges, and the private individuals or members of educational trusts who run independent schools. Each group of providers must somehow take account of the other in the plans they make. Sometimes this taking account is in the form of rivalry and competition. Sometimes there is a tacit reliance that certain groups of pupils will not be turning up in the maintained – or alternatively the independent – schools. They will be catered for by the other sector. Another side-effect of the coexistence of public and private education is the payment of independent schools' fees by local education authorities on behalf of children who have special educational needs or boarding needs which cannot be met in the maintained sector. Later chapters draw on the experience of councillors and officers in two education authorities, and twenty headteachers of independent and maintained schools, to assess the importance of these varied patterns of educational coexistence for the providers of education.

To examine private schools and state schools from the grass-roots perspective of users and providers is scarcely a fashionable thing to do. Most books on education which deal with the private sector continue to be chiefly concerned with the political ideology which promotes or permits fee-paying education (Salter and Tapper 1985, Griggs 1985). This is an important and controversial matter, but it is not the mainspring of interest of my book. In other writings, on the subject of private education, it is the famous boys' boarding schools, the so-called public schools, which are untiringly discussed and dissected (Walford 1984, Fox 1985). These schools are long-standing and influential institutions, but my attention has not been exclusively or mainly focused on them. I have explored the coexistence, alongside local-authority primary and secondary schools, of a whole range of independent institutions – pre-prep and preparatory schools, girls' schools and boys' schools, progressive and traditional, boarding and day. These make up the patterns of educational coexistence with which providers and users of education in the 1980s have to cope – or try to change.

All political parties in the 1980s have policies about the future of private education. These policies are strong on rhetoric but short on sensitivity to the operational implications of what is proposed. They suffer, too, from a lack of recent information on how parental choice is exercised across the public and private sectors of education. My two-year study of these issues, in one corner of southern England, makes a start on filling a large gap.

Robart and Morrowshire are pseudonyms for the two adjacent education authorities which I studied during 1984 and 1985. One is a metropolitan borough, the other a county. Their policies for public education, and the attitudes of councillors and officers to neighbouring independent schools, are examined in Chapter 2. Chapter 3 discusses the local education authorities' use of the independent sector for special and boarding education.

Chapters 4 to 6 focus on the independent schools – their *raisons d'être* and survival strategies, and how the coexistence of the maintained sector impinges on them. Parents come to the fore in Chapters 7 to 9. A number of factors which influence pupil transfer from public to private education are identified, and the notion of a 'threshold of affordability' for fee-paying education is debated. Chapters 10 and 11 sum up the many issues raised by the research and speculate about future forms of schooling.

But before all this can be done, some attention must be paid to the vexed question of political attitudes to the coexistence of public and private education, and an account given of how present-day patterns of coexistence have come about. We turn to this in Chapter 1.

ONE

Private Schools and State Schools: The Politics of Their Coexistence

The coexistence of public and private education in this country is no new phenomenon. Privately funded education predated any national collective provision. But for over a hundred years now[1] central government has assumed responsibility for ensuring that every child has access to a system of schools which are locally maintained and administered. By 1973 eleven years of schooling was compulsory for each child and might be had, without payment, at local schools of the public sector. Nevertheless, private education, for which fees are charged, has continued to be provided alongside the public sector, catering for the same age group. Pupils who attend one of these independent schools during the years 5 to 16 are fulfilling the statutory requirement for compulsory schooling in the same way as if they attended a local-authority school.

In England and Wales 94 per cent of children are educated publicly.[2] Only 6 per cent, on average, have a private education in fee-paying schools. Yet widely varying political attitudes about the continuing existence of the independent schools are strongly held, with a fervour unrelated to the size of the phenomenon.

In the 1980s how people feel about private education is a function of how they feel about public education. An extreme view of public education would be that the institutionalised provision of education is not a proper function for a government: there should be no 'state' schools. This is the 'individualist' view. A directly opposing view would be that public education should be universally provided and exclusively used. There should be a national system

5

of schools (which might or might not be locally administered). It would be both the right and the duty of all children to receive their education at such schools. This is the 'collectivist' position. These polarised attitudes, and the intervening compromise positions, give rise to a range of policies for public education.

At the individualist end of the continuum are the thorough-going 'voucherists', who contend that parental choice should have full sway in a free market of educational provision. Government expenditure on education[3] should go directly to parents to help fund their own plans for their children's education. Next come those who favour a mixed economy for education with a network of publicly funded schools and a range of other independently provided schools, varied in style and level of studies, to which a combination of government support and personal finance would give access. These mixed-economy advocates may be subdivided into those who see the public-sector schools as appropriately meeting the needs of the great majority of children, leaving only specialised and esoteric partialities to be satisfied outside the main educational system, and those 'residualists'[4] who consider that public provision of education should be confined to a bare minimum or should cater only for those who cannot, or will not, supplement public provision by directing personal resources to it.

Moving gradually along the continuum towards the collectivist pole we come to the notion of a fully fledged publicly funded education system, from which individuals are free to opt out provided they embark on some publicly approved alternative. Next comes the idea of public education as a single, universally based system, but one which subsumes various forms of instruction, for example religious and secular. Finally, at the collectivist extreme, we have the state education system as a pure monolith (which might in theory, be either religious or secular). This range of policies for public education is summarised in Figure 1, together with the attendant implications for independent education and for parental choice.

Almost all the six policy scenarios set out in Figure 1 would, in the 1980s, have the support of one or another group within the main political parties (Conservative, Labour, Social Democratic and Liberal). Within the Labour Party the Socialist Education Association (its affiliated education group) favours a development very close to Column 1.[5] Many Labour and Liberal politicians would support Column 2, the Social Democratic Party identifies with Column 3,[6] the Thatcher Conservative government gives support to Column 4 and the right wing of the Conservative Party dallies with Column 6.[7] Some critics would claim that the Thatcher government's education policy in the mid-1980s is such as to move public education towards the position of Column 5, but no political grouping, at present, openly advocates the dwindling of public sector education to a residual role for deprived groups.

Figure 1 shows the implications of this range of views on public education

Philosophical continuum	Collectivist				Individualist	
Policy for public education	Monolithic state system of education	System of state education incorporating secular and religious strands	Public education freely available, meeting most/all educational needs. Individuals may 'opt out' and use independent institutions at their own expense. Central accreditation of these institutions, but no government support for such institutions or transactions	Mixed economy of education (a combination of publicly and independently funded institutions)		No publicly provided education. Public money funding educational 'vouchers' for families. Free market of independent educational institutions
	No opting out			Public education freely available, meeting most educational needs. Some government assistance enabling access to approved independent institutions	Free public education playing only a residual part in the combination (either low level education, or education focussed on deprived groups)	
Column No.	1	2	3	4	5	6
Possible role for independent education	Non-existent		Competitive	Competitive/ Complementary	Complementary	Universal
Implications for parental choice in education	No parental choice (except by moving house to change neighbour-hoods)	Parental choice between secular and faith – linked institutions within the public system of education	Parental choice between public and independent education, but latter option must be fully backed by personal finance.	Parental choice between public and independent education. Full economic cost of use of independent education not borne by family in all cases	Parental choice between public and independent education. Latter option needing to be backed by personal finance, except in selected means tested cases.	Essential for parental choice to be exercised. Possibility of coupling personal finance to public money 'voucher'

for the role of independent education. Leaving aside for the moment any possible intervening external factors, it can be seen that if there were no possibility of opting out of state-provided education, there would be no role for the independent schools as we know them. If opting out was permitted, however, there would be a competitive role *vis-à-vis* the state schools. Column 3 envisages 'no government support' for individuals or institutions involved in independent education, so their situation would be one of 'pure' competition. Not so in the situation of Column 4. 'Government assistance enabling access to approved independent institutions' means that competition would be to some extent muted.[8] If the independent schools chose to specialise in forms of provision *not* available within the public sector, but for which some government support might be available (e.g. special education of children with particular talents or problems), their role could be defined as complementary; that is, rounding out the range of provision available in the public sector. This would be all the more the case should the public sector be reduced to a residual role (Col. 5). And if public education ceased to have any institutional form, the role of the independent schools could be described as 'universal' (Col. 6).

So far the discussion has been in terms of ideas, philosophical attitudes and free-floating policies, more or less uninhibited by notions of legality, feasibility or the experience of practice. All of these latter considerations have played a part in keeping private and public education in a Column-4-type coexistence for over forty years. But established institutions fight back against and mediate policy intentions (Salter and Tapper 1985). Some political scenarios are made well nigh impossible by the presence of impeding institutions which would take many political lifetimes to dismantle. What is it that keeps the heat in the long-running political arguments about the coexistence of public and private education? Why is the subject never allowed to drop quietly from the educational policy agenda, as too difficult to resolve to the satisfaction of all parties, so best left alone? Two points must be clarified: first, what the basis of the argument is *not*, then what it *is* (or has been generally assumed to be).

The argument about the coexistence of private with public education in Britain does *not* have a mainly religious basis, as it does in some other countries. In the United Kingdom coexistence of private schools with state schools is not a coexistence of religious with secular schools. We do not have a secular system of public education. There is no constitutional requirement (as there is, for example, in the United States)[9] for a separation of church and state. All schools provide religious instruction, and public education includes both local-authority and 'voluntary' schools, the latter being schools which are morally and administratively linked to particular religious faiths.[10] And in the same way as publicly provided education in Britain cannot be characterised as secular, the private sector cannot be characterised as religious. In some other European countries, notably France and Italy, private schools are almost without exception confessional (Catholic) schools. In Britain the established church, the Church of England, has its schools within the public sector, and although many independent schools justifiably claim Anglican affiliations (Gay 1985), they do not make up a 'religious sector' of education.

So the arguments about the coexistence of private with public education are not based on religious commitment. It is questions of privilege and social class which have chiefly fuelled the long controversy. These questions have been lengthily debated by writers who have taken equality of educational opportunity as their central theme.[11]

Before the advent of public education, access to schooling was primarily a matter of personal expenditure. The educated few stood out from the unlettered masses. During the first half of the nineteenth century a combination of social and economic changes, with rapid population increase, created new demands and needs for education. Two developments encouraged the separation of educational provision on class lines. The reform and expansion of the great boys' boarding schools gave access for the sons of the increasingly affluent middle class to what has been called 'Tom Brown's Universe' (Honey 1977) – a network of preparatory and secondary schools which in turn gave access to the ancient universities and leadership roles in almost all aspects of social, economic and political life. At the same time, the first systematic attempts were made to provide a basic education for the mass of the population. Two Christian societies – one Anglican, the other Nonconformist – set up local day schools, mainly in the towns. One society had the title 'the National Society for Promoting the Education of the Poor'.[12] Both societies had the poor and hitherto uneducated as their target group. Public education, when it began in 1870, filled the gaps in the network of denominational schools, so as to provide a geographically adequate system of elementary education for the lower classes. Private education, as it expanded, took as its mentors and reference group the famous boarding schools for the sons of the rich and socially aspirant.[13]

These early developments are the basis for the social-class aligned arguments about private and public education in this country. Nothing that has happened in education during the twentieth century has fully neutralised those arguments, but much has occurred to make them less clear-cut. We take up the story in more detail from the 1930s.

Fifty years of developments in educational coexistence

In the years immediately preceding the Second World War the two sectors of education coexisted in a state of almost complete separation from one another. The 1920s and early 1930s had seen repeated attempts by the rising Labour Party, especially in its first two periods of (minority) government, to move towards the introduction of secondary education for all, with its essential accompaniment of the raising of the school-leaving age. These moves had been countered by the alternating Conservative and National

9

governments' policies of severe economic retrenchment during successive periods of acute economic depression. Many aspirations and expectations for the future development of maintained education, and especially maintained secondary education, had been implanted during these inter-war years of political and economic struggle (Parkinson 1970). But the net administrative outcome, by the late 1930s, was that maintained-sector education consisted chiefly of elementary schooling for all to the age of 14.

Some pupils moved out of elementary education at age 11, via the Special Place Exam, popularly known as the Scholarship. These pupils (about 10 per cent of elementary school children by 1939) (Evans 1975, p. 79) went to county grammar schools, where they had to undertake to continue their education to age 16.[14] In areas where there were no or few county grammar schools – and this was particularly the case in the north of England – Scholarship pupils might enter direct-grant schools. These schools, not maintained by local education authorities, had fee-paying pupils and were structurally part of the private sector. However, they received a capitation grant direct from the Board of Education and accepted a proportion of pupils whose fees were paid by local education authorities. Direct-grant schools, sometimes described as a bridge between the private and maintained sector, played an important if increasingly controversial role in secondary education from 1926 (when their relationship with the Board of Education was formalised) to 1976, when their direct funding by the Department of Education and Science was phased out, and most of them continued as unequivocally independent schools.

Elementary education, then, in the years up to the Second World War, was the principal feature of the maintained sector, educating over 90 per cent of the population aged 5 to 14, and educating them free. For those in secondary education the distinction between the public and the private sectors was to some extent blurred by fee-paying practices. The 'special places' won by Scholarship children were means-tested, so that some parents paid a small termly fee for their children's attendance at the county grammar school. A proportion of grammar school pupils were fully fee-paying, not having passed (or in many cases even sat) the Scholarship exam. Their fees were paid by their parents. Those children who were funded by local education authorities to attend direct-grant grammar schools were, in fact, pupils in the independent sector. Some pupils recognised this; others felt themselves to be still in the public sector, and this varying perception of the status of a direct-grant school place continued to colour political and ideological views of education well into the next generation.

On the independent side the well-established direct-grant schools stood shoulder to shoulder with a multiplicity of independent day schools, both preparatory and secondary, which varied widely in educational standards and amenities. Beyond them and most conspicuous, because of their place in the power structure of society as a whole, stood the famous schools, boys' boarding schools which were supplied with pupils from an only slightly less exclusive group of preparatory boarding schools.

Educational coexistence during the war years

The Second World War marked the beginning of a profound change in patterns of educational coexistence, as in many other aspects of the nation's life. Many factors contributed to the strengthening of aspirations for maintained-sector education, encouraged the reaching of a consensus about future policy and ensured the existence of a political will to carry forward the wartime ideas and plans into the realities of peace.[15] One such influential factor was the evacuation of school-children from their home areas.

The evacuation of elementary and secondary school-children were quite different processes. County secondary schools, and also the independent schools, negotiated their evacuation to areas of safety as continuing institutions, and for the most part continued their wartime life as recognisable individual schools, even if subsumed and partly absorbed within a host institution. Elementary school-children were also meant to be kept together as school groups, but the weight of numbers and the need to provide a greater element of supervisory care for these mostly younger children, combined with the eager efficiency of the local health authorities,[16] put paid to that intention. Headteachers who had been placed at the railheads to advise found their advice ignored. Children were divided up into busloads and sent off to different towns and villages, to be billeted in scattered private homes.

Some classmates were eventually brought together again, and received part-time education as a group, in a village hall or some other building. But the process of rebilleting which was needed to bring this about, by accommodating the pupils of evacuated schools closer to each other, proved too great and disturbing a task. Many elementary school-children were out of touch with their original schools, with most of their school-mates, and even, in some cases, with their brothers and sisters if the family was numerous, until they returned home. The experience of evacuation was, for most children, a matter of months rather than years, but its effect on the host communities has been estimated as profound. For the children, too, it was often deeply disturbing.[17]

Along with many other wartime factors, the evacuation of school-children aroused a political will for the future to be improved for deprived families whose life-style had suddenly been made visible in different social communities. The first medium of reconstruction and amelioration was to be education. The White Paper *Educational Reconstruction* was presented to Parliament in July 1943.[18] While it had little to say about the private sector of education (three paragraphs addressed the question of the registration of independent schools), the implications of the document for the future of educational coexistence were far-reaching. The terms of the White Paper conveyed a strong sense of consensus and enthusiasm and a firm intention greatly to upgrade the maintained system of education with particular reference to secondary education. Fee paying was to cease in all maintained schools, and elementary education would be at an end. Every child would be entitled to a free publicly provided primary and secondary education to the age of 15 and later to 16. The maintained sector was standing up to be counted, and taking its first real step away from the status of poor relation to the private schools.

One reason why so little was said about the independent schools in the White Paper may be that there was so much to say about the church schools and their future role in the nation's education. The White Paper of 1943 was, among other things, the outcome of protracted negotiations with the denominational schools, enabling a firm statement to be made about how they could go forward within the maintained system, in a 'voluntary-controlled' or 'voluntary-aided' capacity. This was a real change in coexistence.

Although the White Paper of 1943 did not tackle the question of the coexistence of the maintained and fee-paying sectors of education, it signalled the intention to do so in the near future with the words:

> There remains one important link to forge, between the Public schools and other analagous schools and the general system . . . it is the Government's intention to devise ways and means by which these schools can be more closely associated with the national system.

The following year the Fleming Committee, in their report on *The Public Schools and the General Educational System*,[19] put enormous effort into trying to explain why various parties felt the way they did about these schools and showed that while in 1944 there might be consensus about a brighter future for the maintained sector of education, there was far from being a consensus about either the present or the future of the public schools. Some of the committee obviously valued the schools highly (and knew them well), but a great hostility to the schools because of their exclusiveness was also clearly spelt out in the report.

The Fleming Report stated that:

> the question of associating the Public schools with the general educational system has engaged public interest for considerably longer than the two years during which we have been sitting, but our enquiry is the first systematic attempt made at the request of the Board of Education to formulate concrete proposals for solving the various issues involved.[20]

It was not to be the last such report. The difficulties which the report acknowledged as 'unavoidable in associating two systems which for many years had followed separate paths' proved insuperable on this as on subsequent occasions, and neither of the two schemes for integration put forward by the Fleming Committee was adopted.[21]

Coexistence from 1944 to 1964

In the immediate post-war years the enormous expansion of maintained education required by the 1944 Education Act, and the post-war increase in the child population, pushed questions of unease about educational coexistence to the background for a while. The places which local education authorities were empowered to fund in direct-grant and other independent schools were more than ever necessary now that every child was to receive a secondary education. These places were free to families of low income, and together with the access to maintained grammar schools they enabled a small but delighted section of the population to realise that 'brain not pocket' could get them an academic secondary education of high standard.[22] It is rather scornfully pointed out in a later educational enquiry that 'selective schools were more popular . . . with parents whose children got to selective schools',[23] but the pride and pleasure taken by ordinary families in the academic achievements of their children cannot be written off. During the brief heyday of free selective secondary education in the maintained sector, to be a member of the meritocracy gave guilt-free satisfaction, if only for the few years before sociological research turned a searchlight on the social ingredients of 'brainyness'.[24]

Even before academic selectivity became a sore point in educational discussion, a strength of feeling was growing about 'fairness'. Whereas in the early days of maintained education the private sector, and in particular the famous schools, had some value as an inspiration and marker posts for what schools could achieve, this value declined as the maintained sector embarked on the implementation of its own aspirations for excellence. The well-established fee-paying institutions began to be denigrated as unfair by providers and policy-makers in a sector struggling to establish an adequate secondary education for all. The Fleming Committee, in 1944, had paid little attention to the outcomes of a public-school education, only to its process, and how it might be made available to some children previously educated in maintained schools. The committee's report had acknowledged that throughout the nineteenth century 'those posts which demand a higher education . . . went almost inevitably to persons educated in the Public schools and the older universities'. But gradual change was, the report claimed, 'lessening the predominance' [in such roles] 'of Public school men'.[25] However, the Fleming Committee's analysis did not placate those who challenged the equity of 'jobs for the boys'. By the time the Public Schools Commission began work in 1965, they had to take more explicit note of sustained resentment that a disproportionate number of holders of high office were former public schoolboys, and chronicle the number of vice-chancellors, professors, cabinet members, MPs, air chief marshals, directors, bishops and judges who had benefited from such an education.[26] What has been called 'the politics of envy' cannot be pushed aside as unworthy, any more than the pride of families in new-found academic achievement. It was not until there was at least a possibility that pupils coming through maintained education could graduate to the corridors of power, that the crowding of those corridors by pupils from fee-paying schools began to be objectively assessed. Educational outcomes, and available career paths, became a relevant aspect of educational coexistence.

Educational Coexistence from 1965 to 1979

The year 1965 can be taken as another turning point. It saw the issue of Circular 10/65, which requested local education authorities to prepare and submit plans for reorganising maintained secondary education on comprehensive lines. It also saw the appointment of the Public Schools Commission under the chairmanship of Sir John Newsom, to advise on 'the best way of integrating the public schools with the State system of education'.

The move to ensure that maintained secondary education ceased to be academically selective and became comprehensive was a policy with the potential to change the entire context of educational coexistence, as indeed it proves to have done. Unless the independent schools followed a similar comprehensive line, the maintained sector would henceforward be moving steadily away in a new direction, redefining both the aims and the process of education, and creating an increasing gap between private and state education.

The see-sawing of opinion and action about selective versus comprehensive education which had preceded the issue of Circular 10/65, and the subsequent political moves and counter-moves during the next ten years, mean that any detailed discussion of educational policy over this period has a tendency to become a list of circulars and counter-circulars, reports, appeals and counter-appeals.[27] Nevertheless, in 1965 the die was cast for comprehensive secondary education in the maintained sector, and most local education authorities from that year forward moved gradually towards secondary reorganisation on these lines, whether reluctantly or enthusiastically.

The second watershed event of 1965 was the appointment of the Public Schools Commission, whose task, in the first instance, was to advise on the best way of integrating the public schools with the state system of education. The First Report of the commission, dealing with the public boarding schools was not unanimous, and did not lead to administrative or political action. Nevertheless, it marked the advent of intention to change the public schools (rather than simply make use of them, as the Fleming Committee had proposed to do). The principal thrust of change was to 'reduce the divisive influence which they now exert and bring about a socially mixed entry into the schools'.[28] The social-class-reinforcing aspects of the coexistence of two sectors of education were being publicly articulated and called into question in new uncompromising tones.

The members of the Public Schools Commission were not all agreed on the priority to be placed on social divisiveness. Three dissenters to the report as a whole considered that it placed too much emphasis on this part of their terms of reference and not enough emphasis on meeting boarding need and helping the less able, which were also objectives of the commission. These dissenters found the whole topic of public-school integration beset by 'sterile and excessively doctrinaire controversy'.[29] Some other contributors to the report, however, were singularly determined that, whatever else was achieved, the public schools should be forced to come to grips with poverty in their school populations. In discussing how children should be selected as having a boarding need which would be met by the public schools, they stated, 'it would be right, where priority of need could not be determined on other grounds, to favour the children of poorer parents even though this would have the effect of limiting the number of places . . . or of increasing the cost of integration'.[30]

The question of boarding need, and boarding desire, is still a familiar theme of coexistence discussion in the 1980s. At the time of the Public School Commission's first report, however, the theme was only at the stage of a first reprise. The Fleming Committee had hoped to use the boarding facilities of public boarding schools to benefit boys and girls who would 'learn from Boarding School life the habit of self dependence, of taking decisions and making plans without unnecessary reliance on the guidance or encouragement of their parents'.[31] Since then, the Martin Report had given guidelines of particular categories of boarding need,[32] some of which were beginning to be met in maintained boarding schools. Now it was the turn of the Public Schools Commission to suggest once again that the public boarding schools were in an unrivalled position to meet not only identified boarding need but also hitherto unidentified boarding need, and perhaps also an onrush of populist boarding desire. If these schools opened their doors to boys and girls from low-income families, a whole new section of the population would give serious thought to the characteristics of boarding education and find that they were good.

The majority view of the commission was that there was likely to be need and desire for at least 27,000 new boarding places for assisted pupils in integrated public schools, in addition to the 20,000 boarding places which were already taken up wholly or partly at public expense in independent schools. Even so, one commissioner expressed his dissent, doubting whether there was much unsatisfied demand for boarding education and finding the evidence on which the commission was relying for the measurement of such demand 'tenuous in the extreme'.[33]

Another keynote of the report's discussion was the suggestion that maintained sector education already had something to offer which was superior to or unobtainable in the independent schools. This claim was made on the two counts of co-education and primary schooling.

The possible divisiveness of single-sex education, and the preference of many families for the co-education of their sons and daughters, were raised early on in the report. The commissioners were non-committal about the possible advantages of co-education as a principle of organisation, merely noting that it was more readily available in the maintained than in the independent sector: 'In the maintained secondary sector some 60 per cent of pupils are already in co-educational schools, and we do not know of any evidence that co-education is unsuccessful'.[34] They were more confident, however, in asserting the qualities of maintained primary schools: 'In the opinion of most judges the maintained schools, and not the preparatory schools, are the leaders in primary education'.[35]

For the maintained sector this was a period of great interest in the primary phase of education, with the Plowden Report, *Children and Their Primary Schools*, already in preparation.[36] Twenty years on, in the 1980s, there is a core of doubt among some parents, choosing between private and maintained education, as to whether the state primary schools still have primacy.[37]

One further point of significance remains to be brought out before returning to the main thrust of the commissioners' recommendations. The question of the education of handicapped children in independent schools, with funding from local authorities, was totally excluded from the commissioners' discussions. This aspect of coexistence was implicitly accepted as well established, uncontroversial and to be continued. In the 1980s the terminology has changed and the 'handicapped' are no longer an educational category. But the meeting of some children's 'special educational need' by local-authority funding of places in the private sector, remains a relatively unquestioned feature of educational coexistence.[38]

The overall aim of the commission in addressing the question of the public schools, was to 'build an integrated system of education increasingly close to the maintained sector'. Since the maintained sector was now moving in the direction of comprehensivisation, any 'integrated' system would by definition have to follow. That the public schools should be *socially* selective was a source of long-standing resentment. That they should be highly *academically* selective was a new black mark against them, but one which would count increasingly as selective secondary education was phased out in the maintained sector.

In 1965 comprehensive education, although official policy, was still a matter of hot dispute among educationalists. The commissioners were no exception, and their report acknowledged the profound conflict of ideals about the future direction of secondary education, embracing the problem of how far equality of opportunity was compatible with academic excellence. Two of the commissioners, although they acceded to majority views in signing the report as a whole, inserted a bitter note of dissent about the requirement to bring all the public schools into line with the present policy for all-ability education in the maintained sector. They wanted some highly academic selective public schools to remain. To put a stop to their work would be:

> to level down with a vengeance . . . it should not be assumed that . . . national policy for the maintained sector will remain exactly what it is now . . . if it moves the other way we shall all have cause to be grateful for the survival of this temporarily disfavoured minority.[39]

The report as a whole took the stand that the proposals it made for integration of the public schools with the maintained sector were both feasible (in one or other of the forms they proposed) and potentially acceptable to the public schools. The doubts of some commissioners about the schemes' acceptability to the parties most concerned were however acknowledged by the recommendation that the secretary of state should, 'after every effort of negotiation and persuasion has been exhausted', if necessary ask Parliament 'to give him the powers he needs to compel integration'.[40]

This nettle of compulsion has not yet been grasped in the field of educational coexistence. Without doubt the commissioners knew it was not likely to be, at that stage, for they had already noted their doubt whether public opinion as a whole was ready to support the total abolition of independent schools. There was one other tactic available, the majority proposal that, for 'independent schools which . . . received the greater part of their incomes from sources other than the payment of fees by public authorities or by charities', legislation should withdraw 'the fiscal and other benefits which follow from charitable status'.[41] This proposal too was fated to be held in reserve for many years, as a potential transformer of long-established features of educational coexistence.

The Public Schools Commissioners referred to the Fleming Report of 1944 as a 'dead letter'. Their own First Report on the integration of the public schools, published in 1968, was soon to acquire a similar neglected status. But while this First Report was in preparation, an addition was made to the commissioners' terms of reference. In October 1967 they were asked to:

> advise on the most effective method or methods by which direct grant grammar schools . . . can participate in the movement towards comprehensive reorganisation, and to review the principle of central Government grant to these schools.[42]

This addition to the commissioners' work showed a strengthening of resolve that central government's policy of promoting comprehensive secondary education should be seen to be single minded at central-government level. Whatever delays or objections local education authorities might put in the path of comprehensivisation, they should not be able to say that central government was inconsistent in continuing to direct public funds towards a group of selective grammar schools.

For local authorities and families who at that time had some involvement with both sectors of education, this move to do something about the direct-grant schools had far more significance than any attempt to change the pattern of coexistence with the public schools. Very few children were funded by local authorities to attend one of the famous public boarding schools. But, as the commissioners acknowledged, '5 per cent of school-children in Britain were at direct grant, grant-aided and independent day schools',[43] and many of these held local-authority-funded places. The issue was not so much one of numbers or costs, which were very small in relation to the whole system of secondary education. Rather it was a question of local-authority custom and practice and the forms of secondary education available to local families. In the north of England, especially Lancashire and the West Riding, the direct-grant grammar schools were particularly thickly clustered and were a widely used adjunct to maintained education.

The *Second Report of the Public Schools Commission*, published in 1970, tackled the question of the independent day schools and the direct-grant grammar schools. The commission, now under the chairmanship of Professor Donnison, achieved a unanimous report with few points of formal disagreement (all of which concerned the question of the schools' participation in a comprehensive system). The tone of the report was level, avoiding polemic, but it put its proposals to the schools in 'now or never' terms: 'These schools will never again be able to make so valuable and influential a contribution to the development of secondary education'.[44] Two alternative schemes for participation in comprehensive education were offered to the schools, one funded from central government through a school grants committee, the other entailing assimilation to locally maintained status, possibly on a voluntary-aided basis. But the nub of the matter was that under either alternative the schools would cease to accept fee-paying pupils and would play a comprehensive role, in due course moving to an unselected intake.

The report recognised the likely reluctance of the direct-grant and independent day schools to accept either arrangement. It eschewed any notion of compulsion. The direct-grant schools which did not wish to participate in the movement towards comprehensive reorganisation were free to become wholly independent, with a cessation of public funding. The independent day schools were also free to retain their present status. Local authorities might still fund places at such schools but were urged to do so only when the distinctive contribution of the fully independent schools was 'of a kind that is needed and cannot be provided through the full grant or maintained schools'.[45]

About one-third of schools on the direct-grant list, mostly Catholic schools, accepted voluntary-aided status in particular local authorities, and in due course took part in those authorities' plans for reorganisation on comprehensive lines. But the majority of the schools (some 120 schools) surrendered their direct-grant status and became fully independent. These far-reaching decisions did not however have to be made until five years after the publication of the commissioners' report. During the four years of a fragile Conservative government (from 1970 to 1974) which gave an intermission in eleven years of Labour rule, the schools were able to make their plans.

By 1979 very considerable changes had taken place in the coexistence of public and private education. The direct-grant schools had ceased to exist, and local-authority funded places at former direct-grant schools or other independent day schools had almost all been phased out, following the issue of new regulations.[46] Some 85 per cent of secondary school-children were being educated in comprehensive schools, compared with 32 per cent in 1970. But the whole educational scene now had a new element which would also contribute to change – the phenomenon of falling rolls.

In the era of the Public Schools Commission, expectations about the growth of the education system had been buoyant. Live births had peaked in 1964, and in 1968 the children of this 1960s' 'bulge' were about to enter the primary schools. The *Second Report of the Public Schools Commission* had pointed out that 'in the twelve years from 1968 to 1980 the DES expects 2 million more pupils in maintained schools, 1.3 million of them in the secondary schools'.[47] But live births continued to fall steadily, bottoming out in 1977 at their lowest level since 1941. There were no expectations of a new substantial increase in school-age children for many years, and the maintained sector was faced with reorganising itself to cater for the passage through the schools of a much-reduced child population.

Expectations about available funds for education had also changed during the 1970s. The oil crisis of 1973 had led to cuts in building and spending in all public services, and during the latter part of the decade the costs and effectiveness of maintained education came under increasing scrutiny.[48]

The independent sector, too, had been faced with a possible fall in pupil numbers. The schools had held their own, and there were still 5 per cent to 6 per cent of the school-age population receiving their education in the fee-paying sector, as there had been for many years. But as the 1979 General Election approached, the Labour Party made clear its intention to take the long-awaited step, when returned to office, of removing the charitable status enjoyed by many independent schools.

Educational coexistence from 1979

In the event it was a Conservative government which took office in May 1979. The Thatcher administration, with its market orientation and policies for privatisation, seemed to presage a new era of co-operation for the two sectors of education. The 1980 Education Act introduced a new system of government-funded assisted places in independent schools.[49] When the relationship between public and private education was explicitly discussed in the House of Lords in 1984, during the Conservative government's second period of office, Baroness Young affirmed, 'We do not have two education systems in England and Wales but one . . . enshrined in the Education Act of 1944 . . . it is one system, with two sectors – the maintained sector and the independent sector'.[50]

This was a strong statement by a government spokesman, giving the impression that the clock had been turned back for the coexistence of private and state schools. Yet the consensus of the 1940s no longer prevailed. The whole range of attitudes to public education, described at the beginning of this chapter now had to be reckoned with,[51] together with attendant implications for the role of private education and the exercise of parental choice. To learn more about the phenomenon of educational coexistence in the 1980s, and to see whether private schools and state schools seem like two systems or one, to those who provide and use them, we turn from the normative sphere of policy to the everyday world of practice. How is the coexistence of public and private education experienced by education authorities, headteachers and parents?

TWO

Local Education Authorities and Independent Schools: Councillors and Officers

Morrowshire and Robart are two adjoining local education authorities in the south-east of England – one a county, the other a metropolitan borough. Their joint population is around 1,200,000. In 1984 they provided the arena for my enquiry into how independent education impacted on the providers of maintained education. This chapter explores the views of elected councillors and the ways in which the existence of independent schools influenced the work of officers in the two education departments. In Chapter 3 the reasons why the education authorities bought places in independent schools for special education and boarding education are discussed.

Moving into the local government world of Morrowshire and Robart, in early 1984, first impressions gave no support to Baroness Young's concept of independent schools and maintained schools making up one system of education. About 11 per cent of local children went to private schools, compared with an average of 6 per cent in England and Wales as a whole. But from the point of view of councillors and education officers in the two authorities it seemed that the continuing coexistence of two sectors of education was not a local political issue nor even perceived as a matter of much educational significance.

This had not always been so. Both in Morrowshire, the county authority, and Robart, the adjacent metropolitan borough, some local independent secondary schools had been regularly used by the local authorities for the education of children of high ability. A long-serving education officer in Morrowshire spoke of the former prestige ranking of scholarship places to maintained grammar and, more prestigiously, direct-grant schools, with county scholarships to 'places like Eton' as the pinnacle of achievement. In Robart, too, the authority had formerly taken up many secondary places both in direct-grant schools and in other long-established independent schools in the locality.[1] But no such systematic and regular bridging of the two sectors of education now took place. Following the 1976 Education Act, which in effect made unlawful the use of academically selective independent school places by local authorities, the last LEA-funded places in local independent schools by either authority had been awarded in 1977.

By 1984 these young people had almost all left their school-days behind. For the local authorities the long-standing operational links with the independent sector had dropped away. And while, formerly, education committee members and officers had had reason to interest themselves in the admission procedures and the curricula of certain independent schools, this was no longer the case: 'They are nothing to do with us now' said one councillor. The assisted-places scheme incorporated in the 1980 Education Act had not served to re-establish a link between the sectors, and in the 1980s councillors of all parties seemed content that this should be so. The Education Committee chairman of Morrowshire pointed out that under the new scheme there was 'no financial effect for the authority'. In the economic climate of the time, issues without a financial tag did not typically find a place on policy agendas. Moreover, there was no administrative involvement of any kind for the authority in the new assisted-places scheme. Partners to each arrangement were the independent school, the parent and the Department of Education and Science (DES). In the early stages of the scheme if a 16-year-old from a maintained school was offered an assisted place in the sixth form of an independent school, the agreement of the education committee was needed (and was not always forthcoming in Robart and Morrowshire). But a change in regulations brought this requirement to an end, and in 1984, as one councillor put it, 'we don't know who is going where, so far as assisted places are concerned'.

Local politicians

Although the existence of the private sector was not a prominent political issue in either Morrowshire or Robart, local councillors of each political party seemed to have available as part of their repertoire an expression of principle about private education – principles which were, in some cases, slightly muddied by the councillor's own experience of private-sector schooling. The points of view expressed ranged some way along the philosophical continuum set out in Chapter 1. Nearest to the individualist pole was the education committee chairman in Robart, who held that 'the two sectors can live quite happily side by side. People should have the option to do what they want, including paying for education if they want to – it's up to them.' This point about the freedom of the individual to spend his own money was echoed by the Conservative chairman of the finance and resources committee in Morrowshire. 'If a person has made money which he wishes to spend on his children's education he should be as free to do this as he is to spend it on yachts or chorus girls. If he thinks it's better for his children to go to such a school we should maintain the opportunity for him to make his choice.'

A Liberal education committee member in Morrowshire had valued his own education in the private sector and he, too, stressed that aspect of his party's policy which promoted the freedom of the individual and ruled out abolition of either private education or private health on 'freedom grounds'. But, he said, priority should be given to improving maintained education so that no artificial divide existed between the sectors. A councillor representing the Liberal/SDP Alliance on the education committee in Robart, on the other hand, could not in principle approve of private education because of his objection to élitism.

Two Labour councillors, on the education committees of Morrowshire and Robart, represented the two groupings of opinion within the Labour Party. The Morrowshire councillor was opposed to private education but took a cautious Fabian view of feasible change, and in any case considered that the existence of certain religiously nonconformist independent schools (one of which she herself had attended) clouded the issue about what should be done concerning the existence of private schools. The Labour councillor in Robart, on the other hand, was in no doubt that 'if the nation continues to encourage the private sector we shall educate our future masters by subsidy'. The private sector was as damaging to education as private medicine was to the National Health Service, and was a great danger to democracy. Its abolition 'must be one of the first acts of the Labour Party when they return to power in government.'

These views were expressed in private interview. All the education committee members interviewed in the two authorities confirmed that education committee business never required them to make a stand on their views about the private sector. The Alliance councillor in Robart, recognising that the new assisted-places scheme did not involve the local authority, considered that the scheme had 'let authorities like Robart off the hook, and allowed them not to get involved in a quagmire of contentious debate about supporting the private sector'.

The hard-line Labour councillor in Robart, fundamentally opposed to private education, and an active political campaigner highly experienced in feeding controversial items to the local press, acknowledged that there was no longer political capital in the new assisted-places scheme: 'In local politics there is a need to make effective play on points which are "near home", and attract attention. The new Assisted Places scheme is a dead duck on this count.' This councillor did, however, regularly contrive to draw attention to Labour Party opposition to the private sector by bringing up the question of a particular 'famous' school and its charitable status. The localness of the school gave news value to his complaints, making up for the fact that the Charities Act 1960 was clearly not amenable to alteration by the local authority.

In the opinion of a nominated member of Morrowshire's education committee, who had himself formerly taught in the independent sector, although the ending of the county-funded places or academically selected pupils had cut off some reasons for communication with the private sector, the really big wedge between the sectors had been the comprehensive all-ability schools which now made up the maintained secondary sector. There was now no reason in either Morrowshire or Robart to cultivate links with the private sector – a view shared by the Conservative leader of council in Robart.

However, despite this 'nothing to do with us' attitude by a selection of councillors from all parties in both education committees, all these council- lors confirmed that the committees were regularly asked to make a decision about local-authority funding of individual pupils' fees in private schools. Three justifications for such funding might be advanced: that the child had (1) a special educational need or (2) a boarding need – neither of which, for various reasons, could be met in the maintained sector; or (3) that the child was already a pupil at a fee-paying school but the family had now fallen on hard times. In the latter case the local authority was being asked to ensure continuity of education for the child by meeting or assisting with the school's fees. Because all three types of funding request were individualised and concerned with children in difficult circumstances, it appeared that council- lors did not, in committee, respond to them as political or involving a question of principle. Great reliance was placed on the investigations and recommendations of the officers who had looked into the case before bringing it to the appropriate sub-committee of the education committee. And the complementary nature of the education available in certain private schools seemed taken for granted by councillors in cases where a particular fee-paying place was recommended by officers.

There seemed, for example, to be a general consensus that some ex- perimental and progressive fee-paying schools had a contribution to make in harbouring pupils who could not be fully coped with in the maintained sector. Such pupils might need a small class, or a small school. If the special-services section had gone into a case of special educational need and come up with a recommendation, the education committee chairman in Morrowshire said that he for one 'would not trespass on the professional ground.'

The activist Labour councillor in Robart took the view that individual children should not be used as a way of promoting political views. He expressed complete confidence in the officers in special education, and their recommendations for particular children. Moreover, he would never refuse to 'pick up the tabs' for a family who had fallen on hard times and needed help to keep a child in a private school.

None of the councillors interviewed seemed particularly well-informed about the ways in which boarding need was assessed and met in their authority. Morrowshire had boarding places at two of their maintained secondary schools, and some councillors had the (erroneous) impression that these places would be available for any cases of boarding need identified by officers. In fact, it was rare for any boarding places to be vacant at these schools. Most were taken up by families who themselves paid the boarding fees (although the tuition costs at these maintained schools were of course met by the local authority). One of the schools had a specialised curriculum; the other was voluntary aided, so decisions about admissions to boarding places were a matter for the school governors.

In Robart there were no boarding places at any of the authority's schools. The leader of the council automatically equated boarding education with fee-paying education, implying that borstals were the only maintained boarding schools in existence. Perhaps because any help with fees given by the authorities for boarding need was means-tested (unlike any fee-paying placement for special educational need, for which the authorities were legally required to shoulder the full cost) councillors in Robart did not seem to have put their mind to the question of whether the authority's funding of private-sector boarding places was the only option available. Nor had they recently reviewed the range of criteria officers applied in the assessment and confirmation of boarding need. Slightly garbled versions of the same very unusual case of boarding need were used as an example by several informants in Robart.

Certainly, the issue of boarding need and possible local-authority help for a child in difficult family circumstances to attend a fee-paying boarding school was not seen as politically controversial, any more than the use of private establishments for meeting special educational need. However, while funding of special education in private schools was not objected to on ideological grounds, financial constraints were beginning to cause the fee-paying schools to be increasingly less acceptable, not because they were private but because they were out-of-county. Pressure was beginning to be placed on special-services education officers by Morrowshire's finance and resources committee to recommend placements which would not take money out of the county coffers.

The discussion so far about the meaning of educational coexistence in Morrowshire and Robart has made a number of points, which bear on the subject of central and local government relations. First, local politicians had diverse views – not all strictly in line with official party policy – about the coexistence of the private sector. Various central government actions, whether by Labour governments (removing the direct-grant system and the local education authorities' ability to fund their own assisted-places schemes) or Conservative governments (reintroducing a system of assisted places but *without* local-authority involvement had taken most of the more controversial aspects of coexistence (payments for education on any substantial scale, and academic selectivity) out of discussion. Officers' recommendations about individual cases of need meant that the professionals had by and large removed all the remaining transactions with the private sector from the political decision-making sphere. One reverse trend, on the other hand, bringing back actual financial transactions into the policy sphere, was the 'lumping-in' of private-sector payments with other types of out-of-county payments, and a general policy to cut down on these.

However, it cannot be assumed that because nothing politically controversial was coming to light, the issue of educational coexistence had no relevance at all for the operations of the LEA. We turn now to a more detailed examination of the effect of the existence of the private sector on the work of education officers. As Rhodes (1977) points out, there is never a 'clean slate' in local-authority operations. Past decisions limit today's ability to commit and deploy resources. Patterns of educational coexistence in a local authority are no exception to this general rule. The cases of Morrowshire and Robart illustrate Rhodes's contention.

Local circumstances

Any analysis of educational coexistence at the local level must also take account of the policies of the local authority with regard to its own maintained schools. We have seen that local authorities do not always have clearly formulated and articulated policies with regard to coexistence with the private sector, but they do of necessity have policies about the criteria for allocation of pupils to particular maintained schools, and about the sequential structure of maintained education in a series of schools. The resulting administrative and organisational arrangements for the maintained-sector schools, and the impact which these have on local consumers of education (parents and pupils), are part of the local ambiance within which independent schools exist, and may have an influence on them.

There were a number of similarities between Morrowshire and Robart. Both councils had a long-standing Conservative majority, of a moderate rather than 'True-Blue' coloration. As education authorities they had traditionally responded to the aspirations of local families by emphasising a high priority for the quality of educational provision, through the maintained schools and colleges. Moreover, they found themselves in coexistence with an independent sector which was to some extent common to them both. Parents living in the geographical area, when considering independent schools, were equally likely to consider schools located in Morrowshire or

Robart, or indeed schools closer to the metropolis. The local-authority area in which the family home was situated was irrelevant to their choice, except in the rare cases where the parents were proposing to seek local-authority assistance with school fees. (Enquiries about the assisted-places scheme concerned only the DES, the school and the parents.)

Despite similarities, however, there were a number of particular local circumstances which influenced the way in which the coexistence of the private sector was perceived and responded to in the two education departments.

Morrowshire

In Morrowshire a factor of great importance was the size and complexity of the maintained-education enterprise. The county had been remarkable for its population growth in the 1950s and 1960s, and the population in the county continued to expand from 850,000 in 1964 to 967,000 in 1982. The school population had peaked at 186,000 in 1977. The crude birthrate in the county had, however, been falling since 1965, and by 1982 the school population had fallen to 164,000 and was continuing to decrease.

In 1985 the authority was maintaining 471 primary and middle schools[2] and ninety-three secondary schools, all of which had sixth forms for pupils between 16 and 18 years of age. In addition, there were fourteen major FE establishments, including nine colleges of further education, each of which was close to a town centre in a different part of the county. Most students of these colleges were aged between 16 and 18. The authority also maintained thirty-four special schools.

The countryside of the county could be described as green-belt commuter country rather than deeply rural. Some villages had become affluent, sought-after residential areas. The county also had a number of new towns most of which abutted on to longer-established town areas, but some of the new towns were entirely new areas of post-war development. Because of the pattern of post-war population growth, most of the primary schools were purpose-built for the county's present pattern of primary and secondary education, but there were still some small, old, village-type primary schools, several of which were voluntary aided or voluntary controlled.

The county's secondary schools had widely varying antecedents, and this variety of origin was still apparent in their present-day operations. In the wake of the 1944 Education Act, with its requirement of secondary education for all, the county had provided secondary-school places in a number of newly built schools, but had also expanded inter-war county grammar schools and acquired a number of other secondary schools. At least one of these was listed in the Fleming Report of 1942 as an independent boys' boarding school, but by the 1980s it was a co-educational comprehensive school, part of Morrowshire's maintained sector, still with some boarding places but with many day pupils. In the 1974 reorganisation of local-government boundaries, Morrowshire had absorbed parts of another county, acquiring several of its secondary schools which drew on different county traditions. Voluntary-aided and voluntary-controlled schools were also fairly numerous in the secondary sector. In 1978, 17 per cent of secondary-age pupils in the maintained sector in Morrowshire were in voluntary schools. These included two large, long-established voluntary-aided schools which had acquired new premises in Morrowshire in the mid-1970s, transferring there from another part of the country.

In 1971 Morrowshire's secondary-development plan provided for the gradual reorganisation of all secondary schools on all-ability lines. This reorganisation was deemed to be complete in the 1980s, but two voluntary-controlled, single-sex, former grammar schools were unchanged in name and continued to be perceived as grammar schools by residents over a wide area.

During part of the 1970s Morrowshire, like many other authorities, had operated with a 'hung' council. During this period, consensus had been achieved on certain tenets of education policy which were adhered to when the Conservative Party reacquired an electoral majority. These features of policy were that secondary schools should in all cases cater for pupils on an 'all-through' basis to age 18, and that pupil allocation to schools both at the primary and secondary stage, should be guided first by the criterion of parental choice and only subsequently by logistical or geographical considerations.

As noted earlier in this chapter, Morrowshire had at one time operated a system of local-authority assisted places for secondary education, in what was perceived as a hierarchy of independent schools of varying prestige. This practice was phased out after 1976 but remained part of many families' memory of educational experience.

It was clear, then, that in the 1980s, a time of financial constraint and falling secondary rolls, Morrowshire's education department was faced with running a maintained-education system which had many important assets but also a number of increasingly serious unresolved problems. The tradition of support and encouragement to the exercise of parental choice of school had become coupled with parental expectations that there was much to choose between, in the county's schools. Attempting to close some secondary schools, in the face of such parental expectations, was proving a difficult task. Moreover, at the 16-plus stage the county's all-through schools and its colleges of further education were competing with each other for a dwindling number of students.

How did all this affect education department attitudes to the educational coexistence of the private sector with the authority's schools? In one sense such coexistence could be dismissed as the least of their problems. There was, indeed, a dismissive air about some education officers' comments – 'we scarcely ever think about the private schools'; 'there is no reason for the two sectors to have anything to do with each other now'. As recently as the late 1970s the authority's secondary-development plan had devoted a whole subsection to the independent schools, spelling out education committee policy that the future plans of the independent schools should be taken into account when planning ahead for new or changed maintained school provision.

> Exchange of information including that which may be confidential, should be encouraged in planning for the future . . . The maximum cooperation between schools in the two sectors should be encouraged not only in academic but also in sporting, cultural and social engagements. The independent schools should be taken into account when considering rationalisation, for example at the sixth-form level, or the use of scarce resources.

Reminded of this document in 1985, a senior officer said that changing times had obliterated this vision of fruitful co-operation. People were now working to 'defend the Acropolis'; that is, their own system of education.

Nevertheless, at one level of the local authority's operation the independent schools were still being borne in mind. On the one hand, Schools' Forecasting had to take into account the numbers of Morrowshire children currently educated in the independent schools (a proportion which varied widely in different parts of the county); on the other, it also had to attempt to anticipate ways in which future national and local education policy might affect the balance of pupil numbers in the independent and maintained schools. The way in which this analytic and predictive task was tackled will presently be compared with the approach taken to it in Robart (see the section on assessing pupil numbers, later in this chapter).

Robart

Robart, geographically close to Morrowshire and not dissimilar to it as a unit of local government in political balance and style, was nevertheless a very different local education authority from the shire county. The electoral boundaries of Robart had remained unchanged throughout the twentieth century. Ever since the authority became responsible for the secondary as well as the primary education of its school children in 1944, it had maintained eleven secondary schools to which only two were added over the next thirty years.

The whole maintained-education enterprise in Robart was much smaller than that in Morrowshire. The population of the local authority had fallen from 209,000 in 1961 to 196,500 in 1981. The school population had peaked at 31,900 in 1977 and by 1982 had fallen to 27,990. In 1985 the authority was maintaining fifty-four primary schools, eleven high schools and three sixth-form colleges. In addition, Robart had a college of further education and a college of higher education. The authority also maintained four special schools.

Robart had a tendency to be ahead of the field in its identification and resolution of issues of educational reorganisation. Ever since the three years of a 'hung' council in the 1970s, the local authority's committees, including the education committee, had been constituted from all political parties, though chaired by councillors of the Conservative majority party. To cope with changing educational ideologies and demographic fluctuations, the LEA had played musical chairs with its existing educational premises rather than acquiring new ones. Secondary reorganisation on comprehensive lines had been carried out in 1974 by turning infant and junior schools into first and middle schools, reorganising all the secondary-modern and some grammar schools as four-year high schools taking pupils from 12 to 16, and turning remaining grammar schools into sixth-form colleges. In 1983 falling rolls at 16-plus had led to the closure of one sixth-form college and more recently the closure of one high school had been agreed by the secretary of state. The authority had resolved to move towards the reorganisation of its sixth-form colleges as three tertiary institutions, and put the premises of its college of further education to a different use. Robart was, as has been suggested elsewhere,[3] consensus-seeking rather than conflictual in its mode of operation. During its many phases of educational reorganisation and relocation over the years, the authority had been involved in almost non-stop consultative exercises with its residents and interest groups. Educational reorganisation issues were held in public awareness over such a lengthy period that they became gradually accepted, and even perceived by some as a *status quo ante*. As a result, Robart was, by comparison with many other authorities, one step ahead in its resolution of problems of educational provision.

Education officers

There were a number of ways in which the coexistence of independent schools impinged upon the work of education officers in both authorities. These included the assessment of pupil numbers and the implementation of policy regarding parental choice, including choice of independent schools.

Assessing pupil numbers

In Robart, officers were able to estimate the numbers of pupils being educated in independent schools in the area but had no way of knowing whether those pupils were actually resident in the LEA. The number of school-age residents who began their education in the independent sector was estimated by comparing live births for the appropriate year with the numbers turning up in the maintained schools at the age of 5 or rising 5. Some allowance was made for net migration, and the figures arrived at were averaged over three years to provide an estimate of the proportion of local school-children being educated in independent schools. However, officers readily admitted that the calculation was no more than a rough approximation.

In some parts of Robart there was a noticeable move out of the authority's maintained schools at age 11, one year before the normal age of secondary transfer to high school. This had become so regular a practice that in the authority's 1985 proposed amendment to its primary-development plan, the number of rooms required for one of the middle schools concerned was calculated on the basis that, because of early leaving, only one classroom rather than two was required for the age cohort in the school's final year (11–12 age group). It was assumed that most of these early leavers from middle schools transferred to independent schools, although some were known to move to denominational-aided secondary schools outside the authority, which accepted pupils at age 11. Individual middle schools in Robart were aware of which independent schools their pupils sat entrance examinations for, but the taking up of places in independent schools by former maintained school pupils was not centrally collated in the education department. Central records were, however, kept of how many pupils from independent schools were given places each year in the authority's sixth-form colleges.

It can be surmised that the fairly casual attitude taken in Robart's education department to the loss of middle-school pupils to the independent sector, even though this loss was in some schools as high as 50 per cent of the age cohort, was due to the clustering involved and the fact that the numbers lost would not be sufficient to influence the viability or otherwise of any single high school's population, as each of the middle schools concerned was a 'feeder' to a different high school. Moreover, awareness of any depletion of high-school numbers was counterbalanced by the knowledge of a steady flow in the reverse direction, from the independent to the maintained sector, at 16-plus. In any case, like any other small authority, Robart had to admit and expect that the authority could not conceivably meet the full range of educational need of its residents so some use of other educational provision (whether 'special', single sex or denominational) was inevitable. Because there had always been a lot of movement across the borough boundary (with some adjacent authorities using Robart's schools for their residents while children from Robart in turn crossed the borders to these other authorities), the toing and froing of pupils due to educational coexistence seemed similarly acceptable.

In Morrowshire the coexistence of the independent sector was only one aspect of the authority's problems as far as pupil numbers were concerned. Because of population fluctuation and the operation of parental choice, forecasting future needs for school places was an important function in county hall, and a more sustained attempt was made than in Robart to estimate the part played or likely to be played by the independent sector in catering for local school-children.

Morrowshire had no defined geographical catchment areas on which to base its estimate of likely arrivals in particular schools, and it had long been the county's intention to establish a computerised forecasting system which would be held and updated on the central computer. The main source of data was a centrally held copy of each school's roll, which had been maintained for the past seven years, giving the name and address of each child in a school's pupil population, coded to geographical area. This enabled the recognition of *de facto* catchment areas for each school (i.e. which schools were, in fact, being used by parents residing in a given area), and forecasting was based on these *de facto* areas.[4]

There were several overlapping methods of estimating the number using the private sector. The movement of pupils in and out of the sector were estimated at three stages of school life. The first estimate of '5-year-olds never seen' (and assumed to be attending private schools) was based on the difference between the number of 4-year-olds reported to the county by particular health authorities and the number of 5-year-olds who joined the rolls of maintained or aided schools one year later. Second, drop-out from the public to the private sector at the preparatory stage was estimated by comparing the number of 6-year-olds in the public sector schools with the (hundreds fewer) 7-year-olds in the schools the following year. Third, a similar exercise was carried out to estimate departures at the secondary stage. In order to establish whether leavers were moving away, travelling over the county borders to a school maintained by another authority, or entering the private sector, schools were asked to supply county hall with term-by-term returns of entrants and leavers from their school roll, with details of where the leaver had gone to. And in census years the numbers of resident children in small areas who were attending maintained schools could be compared with the Small Area Statistics available from the Office of Population Censuses and Surveys.

All this overlapping information enabled the county, in theory, to add and subtract a net flow from their original estimate of 5-year-olds never seen in the maintained sector, to arrive at a figure of children in private education. When used as a basis for forecasting, all available figures were averaged over a three-year period to neutralise random fluctuations in annual data.

There were, however, a number of potential sources of error in the data used. Not all health authority figures for 4-year-olds were equally accurate. Over-reporting could occur in areas of high population turnover or through misunderstanding of the naming practices of ethnic minority groups. The destination of pupils changing schools were also in some cases not accurately reported. Those coding the lists did not always know whether the named school of destination was an independent school or a maintained school in another authority.

From the point of view of the county officers carrying out this work, one purpose of estimating how many children were educated in the private sector was to incorporate certain assumptions into the structure-planning review for the next decade. Whereas from raw population projections it might appear that a new primary school would be needed in a particular district by 1996, the estimate for the children of the district typically attending independent schools, for example, might be as high as 25 per cent. If there was confidence in the continuing reliability of this estimate, the county need not embark on land allocation and heavy expenditure for a new school but could plan to accommodate the population increase by adjustments to existing schools. If, however, the local pattern of coexistence of public- and private-sector schools were suddenly to change, whether as a result of political developments or possibly the closure of a local independent school for other reasons, the local authority might have to revise its plan. Whether this would in fact be necessary would depend on how many of the erstwhile independent pupils were actually local residents, entitled to a place in one of the county's schools. The lack of 'match' between local-authority and independent schools' geographical areas of pupil recruitment was a feature of educational coexistence which inhibited planning as well as some potential forms of intersectoral collaboration.[5]

Implementing policy about parental choice, including choice of independent schools

We have already seen that in Morrowshire, by 1984, there had ceased to be any kind of formal relationship at the level of county hall with the independent schools of the area, and this constituted a swing away from the publicly articulated policy of co-operation of 1978. The provision of information or advice to parents about schools in the independent sector was left to the discretion of the various divisional education officers. In the Sesame division, where research activity was concentrated during 1984, the district education officer was prepared to discuss both independent and mantained schools with enquiring parents, and provided a list of independent schools – preparatory and secondary – established in the divisional area. However, it was stressed that this list did not constitute a recommendation.

A very similar practice was followed in Robart. A list of local independent schools was provided to enquirers, and officers were, without prejudice, prepared to discuss with parents the practicalities and problems of transferring a child between the sectors at various stages of education.

Education officers in Morrowshire and Robart made no attempt to dissuade parents from using the independent sector, but they pointed out that the authority was not in a position to recommend particular schools nor to give advice on 'value for money'. Although, as one officer put it, 'one's heart might bleed' for parents who paid fees for a poor-quality independent school and a set of educational resources inferior to what their children would have received in the maintained sector, this was a private matter for the parents.

All officers gave formal backing to their authority's policy of no longer funding assisted places in independent schools except under exceptional circumstances. An officer in Robart who had been working in the authority at a time when the authority offered assisted places in a wide range of independent and direct-grant schools, saw the scheme as having been a desirable and reasonable extension of family choice in which the authority could provide some guidance at that time. But now that the authority no longer had any say in which schools benefited from assisted-place arrangements, it was right that the choice of any school outside the maintained sector should become a private matter for parents. However, if such families continued to live in the area, they continued to be entitled to benefit from all locally provided services. Children's use, for example, of the Robart-funded Saturday music school should not be conditional on attendance at a maintained weekday school. And if, at some future time, parents wished to move their children back into the maintained sector, they should not be 'punished', by officer disapproval, for having used an independent school. Any question of *priority* of access to, for example, Robart's sixth-form college by students from independent schools was a politically touchy issue, and any such impression of priority was to be avoided. But there could be no justification for defining pupils from independent secondary schools as ineligible to enter a sixth-form college maintained by the authority. As local residents they had the same right to local-authority provided education as any other resident.[6]

An officer in Morrowshire regretted that parental expectations about the desirability and feasibility of school choice had been greatly heightened by central-government attitudes and statutes. Now that parents had a statutory right to stipulate the maintained school of their choice, and knew of the existence of formal appeal procedures, there was an impression that they *should* exercise such a choice. Over a period of years parents in Morrowshire had appeared to be coming to the conclusion that all the authority all-ability schools were of a good standard, and there was no need to decide on schools for reasons other than those of geographical convenience. Since the introduction of new formal arrangements backing the parental choice which had always been available to Morrowshire parents, however, a pecking order of desirable schools had become established in parent's minds. Parental choice had began to cluster on a small group of maintained schools which appeared to have something distinctive about them. If over-subscription to such a school meant that a place was not available, parents would turn to the independent sector, creating a situation where less-popular maintained schools sometimes experienced rapid and disproportionate decrease in their pupil rolls, due to low intake.

The question of whether local authorities should 'market' their maintained schools in any co-ordinated exercise in public relations, so as to focus parental choice on the maintained sector, did not appear to have been seriously addressed in either Morrowshire or Robart. Both authorities stressed the autonomy of individual schools, and left it to each school to make its own arrangements to welcome or attract the interest of local parents. The requirements of Section 8 of the 1980 Education Act for schools and local authorities to provide information about each school had been complied with. But, as one officer in Morrowshire pointed out, 'the independent schools are streets ahead of us with their brochures and so on'. In Sesame division of Morrowshire, a booklet called *Secondary Schools*, issued under the auspices of the county's education committee, and prefaced by a letter from the divisional education officer, was available to parents. Each of the schools concerned had evidently prepared its own contribution and submitted it for inclusion in whatever typeface and with whatever sub-headings and format it felt appropriate. Some accounts were illustrated with black-and-white drawings or drafted in the form of questions and answers. Others were exhaustive formal accounts of every detail of subject choice and school dress requirements. The booklet as a whole gave no sense of a co-ordinated overview of available secondary provision and did not enable systematic comparison between the schools. Nevertheless, it did give some flavour of the individuality of the schools, and gave credence to the county's claim that each school enjoyed considerable autonomy. In the matter of allocations of places, or pupil recruitment, however, the logical purpose of any public-relations information exercise, the maintained schools had little or no control over who joined their rolls.

Education officers' own views on private schooling

The question of whether education officers should or will voice a personal opinion which is contrary to that of the current policy of the educational committee probably depends on the temperament and seniority of the officer concerned. One senior officer was quite clear that while he would pursue the education committee's policies, he would make known his own opinion if this differed from the prevailing view. In due course policy might change, and although it was 'one thing to be hoist with your own petard, there was no reason to be hoist with someone else's'. It did, however, appear that the interpretation of contemporary educational coexistence as a situation in which the maintained and independent schools were following separate paths, with the maintained sector stressing comprehensive all-ability pro-vision, was an interpretation with which most officers in both Robart and Morrowshire were in full professional agreement. Some officers had been educated in or at one time taught in independent schools, but for the most part there was a sense of provenance from and personal experience of the maintained sector which differed sharply from the educational ambiance of officials at the DES. In line with education committee attitudes, officers in both authorities appeared to have a 'live and let live' attitude to the private sector, but there was no propensity to foster intersector involvement. One officer in Robart confirmed that in a time of falling rolls and education cuts there was 'no will from the department to encourage councillors to decimate the maintained system by any kind of local assisted-place scheme' – but he pointed out that some headteachers seemed prepared to encourage their leavers to move off in the direction of the private sector.

In summary, officers' attitudes to the coexistence of the independent sector seemed to be that it provided competition of a fairly irrelevant kind. The independent schools were providing an education which did not specifically complement the comprehensive approach of the maintained schools but was one from which each authority had already moved on. Although some parents might prefer and chose an independent school for their child, this was not seen as a trend which should influence the education authority in the type of schooling it now provided, nor was the departure of some children to the independent sector seen as depriving the maintained schools of able young-sters who had been good 'markers' for school achievement. In individual cases education officers took the professional line – 'whatever is in the best interests of the child'. Questions of the competitive or complementary situations of the two sectors of education were set aside when an individual child's educational path was in question. This individualised response to the public issue[7] of educational coexistence was similar to that which had taken place at the level of local policy-makers.

THREE

Local Education Authorities and Independent Schools: Special Education and Boarding Education

Whatever their own views on private schooling, education officers have regularly looked to the independent sector to meet certain needs of individual children through special education and boarding education.

Special education

Throughout England and Wales, since 1944, the majority of pupils who need special help with their education have had their needs met in maintained special schools. But the maintained sector of education has never aspired to make provision for the special educational needs of every child. It has always been recognised that some highly specialised needs can only be met, with any degree of economic efficiency, by individual private institutions. However, the 'special education' interests of the private sector in the 1980s were not confined to a handful of schools catering for pupils with rare disabilities. They also comprised a substantial number of 'non-maintained special schools'[1] and a plethora of small independent schools set up to meet the needs of pupils defined as maladjusted, now known as 'emotionally and be-haviourally disturbed', or EBD.[2] There were also a number of independent

37

schools which accepted into their pupil populations a small proportion of children with special educational needs.

The non-maintained special schools were those institutions of education, for children with particular types of handicap, which were established as part of voluntary charitable effort to help people with certain obvious and severe forms of disability. No clear-cut definition of the 'non-maintained special school' was in common use in the 1980s, but occasional descriptive references to the schools were to be found in government publications. One such description stated:

> Non-maintained special schools are run by voluntary bodies; they may receive some grant from the department [of Education and Science] for capital work and for equipment but their current expenditure is met primarily from the fees charged to LEAs for pupils placed in the schools.[3]

DES Circular 6/83, concerning the approval of special schools, pointed out that most of the non-maintained special schools were regulated by trusts. Those of the non-maintained special schools which dealt exclusively with pupils within a single category of handicap (such as schools for the deaf or blind) had usually been created by societies which constituted interest groups concerned with the disability in question. These interest groups worked closely with Her Majesty's Inspectorate (HMI) and were very much part of the 'establishment' in special education.

A number of completely independent schools also catered for children with special needs. Until 1978, when 'recognition' of independent schools was discontinued, all independent schools accepting children with special educational needs would have been on the 'recognised' list.[4] Following the implementation of the 1981 Education Act in 1983, HMI began a special programme of inspections of the relevant independent schools, with a view to drawing up a list of schools which wished, and were eligible, to be known as 'approved' for special education purposes. However, whether or not an independent school receives the formal approval of the secretary of state, permitting it to be used for the placement of children with statemented special needs,[5] it is incorrect to refer to it as an independent special school. There is no such institution as an independent special school. All schools formally known as special are either maintained or 'non-maintained'.

Some independent schools (like Culinara and the Philosopher's School, described in the next chapter) regularly accepted pupils with special educational needs, whose fees were paid by the local education authority. Such schools, however, which did not wish even informally to be known as independent special schools, did not seek blanket approval by the secretary of state for the placement of such pupils. They were content for each individual case to be submitted for *ad hoc* approval. The largest category of independent schools taking pupils with special needs were those equipped to accept maladjusted pupils. In a list of non-maintained and independent schools used by thirty local education authorities in the south-east of England in the early 1980s,[6] 90 per cent of the listed schools used for maladjusted children were fully independent.

Whether an education authority is small, like Robart, or large like Morrowshire, it can confidently be stated that some of the special educational needs of its children will be met outside the maintained sector of education. The pattern of use made of independent schools depends, however, on the range of special education provision made by the authority itself, and the experience and expertise of the professional specialist practitioners and advisers working in the authority, as well as the administrative and political tenents adhered to by officers and elected members.

Officers working in Robart in the 1980s considered that the authority would be accurately described as 'easy-going' in its administrative practice, compared with other larger authorities. Particularly in the field of special educational need, a traditionally non-politicised aspect of education, decisions would be influenced and fairly readily swayed by any strongly held preference of an interested party. The authority had only three special schools of its own, the two largest of which were for ESN(M) and ESN(S), whilst the smallest of the schools was for the 'maladjusted' category of pupil. On average, during the five years preceding the implementation of the 1981 Special Education Act (in 1983) 30 per cent of the children in Robart who were on registers for some form of special education were being paid for by the authority in non-maintained or independent schools. The comparable figure for Morrowshire was 10 per cent.[7] Morrowshire had over thirty maintained special schools including a number of specialist establishments.

The school population as a whole, in both Robart and Morrowshire, had been falling sharply since 1977, and it might have been expected that pupils receiving special education would show a proportional decrease. Nevertheless, during the four years from 1979 to 1982 inclusive, the number of children on-registers for all types of special education provision in Robart stayed constant, and in fact showed a small increase of 3.5 per cent over the four-year period. The 'on registers' figure for Morrowshire showed a 15 per cent decrease over the same period. In Morrowshire pupils awaiting or registered for special education provision as maladjusted decreased by 23 per cent between 1979 and 1982. Morrowshire made use of maintained boarding education for some of its maladjusted children, and this figure decreased by 9 per cent in the four years. In contrast to these decreases the number of maladjusted Morrowshire children in independent boarding education increased by 2.25 per cent. In Robart the number of children awaiting or registered for special education provision as maladjusted *increased* by 22.5 per cent (compared with Morrowshire's 23 per cent decrease over the same period). Robart made no use of maintained boarding education for maladjusted children during those years. The number of maladjusted children Robart placed in independent boarding education increased over the

Table 1 Changes in the placement of children with special educational needs in Morrowshire and Robart (1982 figures as a percentage of 1979 figures)

	Morrowshire	Robart
On registers for special education of all kinds	84.82	103.50
All awaiting or on registers for malad. special education	76.69	122.60
Maintained malad. boarding education	91.12	—
Independent malad. boarding education	102.25	214.28

four years from 1979 to 1982 by no less than 114 per cent. These comparative changes are summarised in Table 1.

It is evident that the figures in Table 1 were affected by many more factors than falling rolls. Special education numbers in Robart appeared to be expanding to fill the places available while in Morrowshire they were declining overall in line with falling rolls. Maladjusted numbers seemed to be a special case in both authorities, particularly as far as boarding places at independent boarding schools were concerned. They showed a slight increase in Morrowshire and an enormous one in Robart, indicating that this form of educational coexistence was proving increasingly useful in the field of special education, during the period immediately preceding the implementation of the 1981 Act (in 1983).

The research took place too soon after the implementation of the Act to show what effect new procedures would have on overall numbers of children receiving special education. In the first year both authorities found that the many consultative stages of 'statementing' slowed up the placing of children on all types of register. New forms of administrative record, in line with the spirit of the 1981 Act, ceased to place children in categories so that the 'maladjusted' or 'EBD' pupils were no longer identifiable as an official group (although authorities no doubt continued to group cases for their own information). Officers in both Robart and Morrowshire confirmed that the need to seek the secretary of state's approval for individual placements in independent schools not yet on the HMI 'approved list', or at schools which were not seeking blanket approval, was slowing up the placement of children at such schools even more markedly. Some of the independent schools with tight budgets were concerned to find that by August 1984 they did not yet know how many pupils would be sent to them by local authorities in September 1984. An officer in Morrowshire commented that one effect of the new 'approval' procedure was to encourage conservatism in the choice of independent schools. New experimental placements were less likely to be made, however promising a new or hitherto untried independent school might look in the provision it offered for children with special educational need.

Another influence in changing patterns of use of the independent sector by local authorities in the 1980s was unequivocally financial. Hard times in maintained education – and in local-authority finance generally – were influencing many aspects of administrative practice. Local-authority expenditure on independent education was no exception here. Morrowshire, a large authority, had begun to cut down on out-of-county educational expenditure of all kinds, and the use of independent school places, for whatever form of specialised need, came under similar scrutiny. In Robart, however, it was still the case that, with the small number of cases generated in a small authority, no economy could be effected by attempting to meet specialised forms of educational need within the borough. It was cheaper to buy a place than to provide it. So far as the more numerous EBD pupils were concerned, however, Robart too was becoming increasingly reluctant to pay for these pupils to attend independent schools. Termly fees were high and payable in advance. If a volatile EBD pupil absconded during the term, a fairly frequent occurrence, independent schools did not refund fees. In similar circumstances in an out-of-county maintained school, only a *pro rata* charge would be made to the user authority.

Relatively minor financial considerations of this kind played a part in influencing use of the independent sector during a period of general economic contraction. They were also leading some authorities, including Robart, to create some new forms of day places for special educational need, using space made available by falling rolls within mainstream schools. These new places were not perceived as a response to pressure for 'integration' of special-needs children into mainstream schools.[8] Rather, they were considered to be an economic use of existing resources, and philosophically attractive in that the children were educated close to home. However, officers in both authorities thought it unlikely that provision for emotionally and behaviourally disturbed children would ever be fully made on a maintained basis. The requirements for such provision were generally costly – small numbers of children per school and a high ratio of professional attention, including the availability of a psychiatrist, were among the requirements. Moreover, unless political developments radically changed patterns of educational coexistence, any new maintained school for EBD pupils would be competing with the large number of long-established and experienced independent schools for this type of child.

Decisions about placements

Officers' decisions about placements are meant to take account of all views, including those of parents. Theoretically, the decision as to which school will best match the 'statemented' educational needs of the child is made from a range of schools limited only by the authority's knowledge of the school's existence and the type of provision it makes. In practice, as we have seen, the range within which choice is made might be restricted by a policy regarding the limitation of out-of-county expenditure, or the confidence based on experience that placements at certain schools were likely to receive the approval of the secretary of state.[9] In some authorities, officers might have discretion to authorise the placement of a child at one type of school, but sanction by elected members might be needed for other types of school. For example, in Robart a placement at an independent school informally defined as a 'special' school could be authorised by the education officer in charge of special education. But if a placement was recommended at an independent school which, although it accepted some pupils with special educational need, did not deal exclusively with such pupils, this recommendation would have to go before an all-party group concerned with pupil admission. Having the recommendation considered at this working-group level was, however, seen by the education officer concerned as an advance on previous practice. Formerly, recommendations had had to go before the Schools' Sub-committee, where opinions about the issue of using independent schools were always aired on party-political lines before the individual case was considered on its merits. In other larger authorities, such as Morrowshire, all recommendations would be submitted to the appropriate committee, but as a prominent majority-party councillor in Morrowshire pointed out, 'in special education emotion overrides anything else – it is not a political issue'. However he followed this remark by pointing out that, nevertheless, out-of-county places were in future going to have to be restricted.

One great advantage of using out-of-county maintained provision for educational need, rather than independent provision, was that Assistant Education Officers (AEOs) could have recourse to one another for advice about the quality of the school concerned. 'The AEO knows everything about his schools', one officer claimed. But there was no network of contacts in the private sector to which an officer could go for a view on particular schools. The need for some objective standard of professional appraisal was keenly felt. Local-authority education advisers had no jurisdiction in independent schools. HMI were the only people who could be turned to, and their knowledge of the whole range of independent schools was incomplete. If there was something wrong in a private-sector school, one might only find out through the pupils; for example, from comments made by a pupil to the education welfare officer detailed to escort the child home at the end of term.

Educational psychologists in a number of local athorities were consulted by one another about independent schools they visited or used. These exchanges of professional information were confidential and informal. At one time user-authorities, including Robart, had circulated written appraisals of particular schools, but this had been discontinued when the headteacher of a criticised independent school complained that this practice affected the livelihood of independent school providers, without the possibility of appeal.

It was not the role of the educational psychologists to recommend a specific school at which a child should be placed. Their contribution was intended to be a professionally based description of the child's needs, regardless of what kinds of provision existed for those needs to be met. Officers in both Morrowshire and Robart accepted that in fact psychologists' recommendations did take account of available resources. They considered this to be inevitable and also to some extent the reason why the budget limits for special education had never had to be tested. Educational psychologists' recommendations were also influenced by their own knowledge of schools, both independent, maintained and non-maintained. They built up this knowledge by visits and by discussion with educational psychologists in other authorities. No independent school was ever used for the first time without a visit being made, but authorities varied in the extent to which they continued to make review visits to schools where only one or two pupils from an authority were placed. Given that the independent schools meeting special educational needs were small and numerous,[10] manpower resources were the main restriction on psychologists' visits.

Dyslexia and the local education authority

As we have seen, a number of factors influenced the decisions taken by education officers about the school in which a child's special educational need could appropriately be met, whether in the public or the private sector of education. But there was one group of cases where the definition of need was itself seen as debatable – children described as dyslexic. Neither in Morrowshire or Robart was there a clear policy that the local education authority would itself provide treatment for such children within its own schools (whether mainstream or 'special'). Nor did the local education authorities seem prepared to fund the education of dyslexic children in independent schools. Parents, local authorities and voluntary teachers from the dyslexia interest-group were, by largely informal negotiation, arranging a temporary blending of public and private education. Voluntary teachers from a local dyslexia unit came into maintained schools to give children individual tuition, and payments were made to the unit in some cases by parents, in others by the authority. It was hard to say whether this compromise situation was chiefly influenced by professional reservations about the nature of the dyslexic disability, or by the financial implications for the local education authority of giving full-blown recognition to a new form of special educational need.

Dyslexia, which was at one time called 'word blindness', can be described as a language processing problem. Dyslexics find it difficult to remember letter sequences, but there are degrees of handicap. Some can read fluently, with symptoms only appearing in spelling forms. Others read much more slowly and find difficulty in copying notes. Severe sufferers produce mirror writing.[11]

Like most voluntary associations, dyslexia interest-groups had founders from the middle class, and this enabled opponents of the movement to define it as special pleading by the middle classes for their slow-learning children. In 1984 an education officer in Morrowshire commented that dyslexia seemed to be an acceptable kind of educational need from the point of view of parents. To say that a child was dyslexic rather than dull was preferred by parents. In fact, in some cases a child might equally well be defined as having 'moderate learning difficulties'. This view represented one widely expressed response to pressure-group activity concerned with dyslexia, but some other professionals in education were prepared to acknowledge the existence of an identifiable problem. Insofar as the dyslexic condition had in the early 1980s received any official recognition, it was referred to as 'a specific learning difficulty'. Its causes were variously defined as emotional problems deriving from family life or hereditary. In 1985 the neuropsychology unit at the Radcliffe Infirmary, Oxford, received funding from the Medical Research Council for a new programme of research into cases of dyslexia. Other pieces of research were also in progress,[12] and the problem seemed to be becoming accepted as 'a medical condition rather than a middle-class apology for stupidity'.[13]

In earlier years the coexistence of public and private education appeared to have been a divisive factor in the development of dyslexia pressure-group activities. Perhaps because of the relatively minor nature of the handicap – a troublesome and disturbing hindrance to a child's educational advancement, rather than a major bloc to normal mental and emotional development, such as, for example, autism – dyslexia was a learning difficulty which created a 'market' for treatment. Some groups found it natural to look to the private sector, seeing dyslexia as yet one more specialism which could fitly be provided on an independent basis, with most costs being met by individual families but with systematic attempts to tap into local-authority resources for financial assistance with some cases. This was one classic way in which many types of special educational need had over the past years been met through independent education, with the family purse being opened by the force of the parents' anxiety about their child.

An alternative response was the strategy of extending the scope of *maintained* educational provision, so as to deal with the newly identified specific learning difficulty of dyslexia. Specialist teachers (privately trained) would first come into the maintained school to demonstrate what could be achieved by specialist tutoring, then steps would be taken to make training available for interested teachers in the maintained sector, a training which extended their professional skills and the range of need which they could meet within the school and which could be incorporated into the recognised accreditation system with which teachers in the maintained sector were already familiar.

This latter strategy was the one being followed by the Prospect Dyslexia Unit, a voluntary group geographically based in Morrowshire. The director of the unit, a teacher who formerly taught in maintained schools, had as her aim the eventual 'withering away' of the unit as its functions were taken over within mainstream education. To this end it was important for the unit to rent local education authority premises rather than private premises for its base to emphasise the unit's close connection with the authority. The county's chief education officer had been prevailed on to open the first premises in which the unit was housed, in a disused school, and protracted negotiations with the authority had subsequently made possible a move to occupy two rooms in a primary school. This was all part of the unit's general policy to 'infiltrate' the maintained educational system. The unit was administered from its base premises, and some teaching took place there, but the preferred mode was for lessons to be given by unit teachers to dyslexic children in school hours at the maintained schools they attended. With the tacit or explicit agreement of several authorities, arrangements of this kind were individually negotiated with headteachers of schools throughout Morrowshire and some adjacent areas, including Robart.

In Morrowshire parents paid the unit for lessons in school hours and on school premises (and there was a similar practice with regard to individual music lessons). Some officers at county hall were diplomatically unaware of this contravention of the 1944 Act,[14] and the director of the Prospect Unit was content that this should be their attitude. All political parties on the council were favourably disposed to the unit, and dyslexia was not a political issue. If any furore arose about payments for teaching done within maintained schools, the more widespread music teaching would be the first target. There was no point in insisting that officers acknowledge private provision of teaching for dyslexic children which the authority itself was not in a position to fund. In any case, fees were remitted by the unit to needy parents on an individual, flexibly discretionary basis.

In Robart, however, the question of payment for in-school teaching of dyslexic children had been formally raised in the education committee, and the authority's former 'blind eye' policy had come to an end. Unit teachers no longer gave lessons in primary schools, but their teaching in secondary schools continued and was funded by Robart. This policy too was acceptable to the unit, on the principle that it was important to remain on good terms with the local education authority and accept the kind of access to schools which the authority found politically feasible at the time. Meanwhile, dyslexia activists were collaborating with the Royal Society of Arts to set up a diploma course for teachers working with individuals who were 'underfunctioning because of specific learning difficulty with literary skills'. If and when DES poolability was achieved for the course, it could be funded from the DES central pool for teacher training, with the possibility of acquiring the same status and widespread availability as the diploma for teaching English as a second language (ESL).

In 1985 a high-court judgement ruled that a gifted dyslexic boy had special educational needs.[15] The judge quashed the earlier decision of a local education authority that the boy was not entitled to attend an independent school with special facilities for dyslexic children. The authority had a mandatory duty under Section 6 of the Education (Miscellaneous Provisions) Act 1953 (as amended by the Education Act 1980 and 1981) to pay the whole of the fees when special educational provision was required in an independent school. This case was of interest and encouragement to both wings of the dyslexia movement. From the point of view of those orientated towards the maintained sector, it was a welcome reinforcement of the idea that dyslexia was a disability requiring a particular teaching response which did not come within the scope of broadly remedial teaching as presently perceived. Rather than pay for such children to attend independent schools, authorities might become increasingly enthusiastic about the provision of accredited diploma courses in local institutions and the secondment of teachers to such courses.

From the point of view of those interested in meeting the needs of dyslexic children through independent education, the judgement was even more directly encouraging. By its recognition that a particular dyslexic child had special educational needs, it opened the door to full funding by local authorities of the education of children with such needs, whether in independent or maintained schools. The many independent schools which had begun to specialise in the education of dyslexic children could have increased confidence that, subject to the school's approval by HMI, or the agreement of the secretary of state in individual cases, a new source of supply of pupils for whom fees could be met would open up. Those chiefly dealing with dyslexic children through the independent sector of education did not anticipate that specialised institutions would 'wither away' as the disability became more widely acknowledged.

Boarding education

The extent to which LEAs become involved in paying for children's boarding education, on grounds of 'boarding' need is very much smaller than their involvement in financial transfers to non-maintained and independent schools in respect of children's 'special educational' needs. This is not to say, however, that large sums of public money are not devoted to payments for boarding education, both in independent and maintained schools. But the majority of such financial transfers go directly from central government, via families, to the schools, in the form of boarding-school allowances for children whose parents are in the armed forces or the diplomatic service.[16] In this chapter our concern is only with the role of *local* government in funding specialised forms of education, including boarding.

At the time of writing, there are no definitions of boarding need which have statutory power. However, the guidelines used by most authorities since the 1960s are those in the *Report of the Working Party on Assistance with the*

Costs of Boarding Education, 1960, generally referred to as the Martin Report. The report recommended local authorities to give favourable consideration to applications for help with boarding education which fell into one of four categories:

(i) Cases in which both parents were abroad;
(ii) Cases in which the parents were in England and Wales, but liable to frequent moves from one area to another;
(iii) Cases in which home circumstances were seriously prejudicial to the normal development of the child;
(iv) Cases in which a special aptitude in the child required special training which could be given to the child only by means of a boarding education.[17]

The assistance which the recognition of boarding need was intended to trigger was the means-tested payment of boarding fees for the child or children in question. Local authorities already accepted responsibility for the tuition costs entailed in the primary and secondary education of every child in the land, and through recoupment arrangements could secure reimbursement for the cost of educating any child who, for one reason or another, went to school outside the 'home' local authority. The 1944 Act's stipulation of free education meant that these costs were met in full. But because of the high costs of boarding education, boarding fees were only to be met by local authorities on a means-related basis.

The 1944 Education Act had also enjoined local education authorities to 'have regard to the expediency of securing the provision of boarding accommodation, either in boarding schools or otherwise, for pupils for whom education as a boarder is considered by their parents and by the authority as desirable'. A number of maintained boarding schools and boarding places at maintained day schools were subsequently established. In the 1980s boarding places and boarding schools existed in both sectors but they were still infinitely more numerous in the independent sector – at least 130,000 places in the independent schools in 1983, compared with some 10,000 places in the maintained sector (Dennison 1984, p. 75).

In both Morrowshire and Robart, particular education officers had responsibility for handling claims of boarding need and making recommendations to the appropriate committees about whether individual claims should be admitted. This task was usually a minor part of their overall responsibilities. In a small authority like Robart, only a handful of claims resulted in local-authority funding each year, and in Morrowshire numbers were only proportionately greater. But almost all of these authority-funded boarding places were likely to be in the independent sector. Robart had no boarding places in its maintained schools, and in Morrowshire, as already noted, boarding places in the county's two schools which had residential provision were usually already filled by parents who paid the boarding fee

47

themselves (sometimes with the help of a Services boarding-school allowance). In any case, as a rule, parents who successfully applied to the local education authority already had a particular independent school in mind, especially if their claim was made under the Martin Report's fourth criterion (of special aptitude).

Because of steep rises in fees in independent schools, and especially in the costs of residential schooling, a much harder look at cases of boarding need was being taken by officers in both authorities. At the same time it was recognised that a case defined as 'boarding need' would be means-tested and might cost the authority substantially less than a full-blown case of 'special educational need'. Moreover, in Morrowshire, there was a top limit on what could be paid for boarding education by the authority, regardless of means-tested eligibility. This top limit was considerably lower than contemporary boarding costs, so that even when boarding need had been recognised, a family might be unable to afford the gap between costs and what the authority could offer, and hence be unable to take up the boarding place available. By contrast, there was a statutory obligation on all authorities to meet in full the tuition *and* boarding costs of a case of special educational need, duly 'statemented'.[18]

For the education officers concerned, the chief problem in making recommendations about boarding need, especially on social grounds (Martin Report, third criterion), was the subjective nature of the judgments being made. In the absence of a medical or emotional symptom on the part of the child (which might have justified appraisal for special educational need), one was attempting to form an opinion on the quality of family life, and whether this might be prejudicial to a child's progress in a day school.

Although the private sector was usually the destination of a child whose boarding need was acknowledged by the local education authority, officers in Morrowshire and Robart found that committee responses to their recommendations were not made from polarised political positions. Both parties seemed to have settled for focusing on the needs of the child, and the pros and cons of giving a boarding place were discussed in individualised terms. However, the preparation and presentation of individual cases, each settled on an *ad hoc* basis, were seen as making heavy demands on officers' time.

Nevertheless, the role of the local authority in funding boarding education must be seen as a relatively minor involvement. The great majority of parents who want boarding education for their children pay for it out of their own pockets. Another substantial grouping looks to the Ministry of Defence for financial assistance rather than the local authority. As with the assisted-places scheme, so with boarding education, the public funding of large numbers of places in independent schools is currently outside the local education authority's remit.

FOUR

The Independent School and Its Raison d'Etre

So far we have seen something of how the independent schools looked from the viewpoint of the local education authorities – how they were for the most part irrelevant, but sometimes a useful destination for children with particular educational needs. Now we turn to the independent schools themselves, to examine their purposes and whether their headteachers see the maintained sector as competitive or complementary to their own endeavours.

The so-called independent 'sector' is made up of so many different types of independent schools that their headteachers do not typically see their institutions as part of a system which includes all non-maintained schools. Some of them recognise a common purpose with certain other independent schools; others see their own school as a unique unit.

For the headteacher of an independent school, his or her school must have a *raison d'être* which justifies the school's continued existence. In the maintained sector this is less necessary at the level of the individual school. It is the policy of the local education authority which keeps the maintained school in being, and although the headteacher may well have distinctive aims for the school, these must tie in with the requirement to meet the general educational needs of a particular age cohort within the population. The denominational schools at one time stood between these two positions, in that each group of the religious schools had a corporate *raison d'être*, to provide education with a particular religious basis, but in becoming voluntary-aided or voluntary-controlled they joined the educational 'establishment' and became committed, at the least, to taking account of local education policy and, at the most, to being guided by it.

The independent sector has no overarching corporate existence, hence no corporate *raison d'être*. The various associations to which independent schools

49

are affiliated are often thought to provide a unifying infrastructure for the private sector.[1] But contacts with the administrative side of some of these organisations indicated that the autonomy of individual heads was held in great respect. Membership of an association by no means entailed the uniformity which outside observers sometimes attributed to, for example, schools of the Headmasters' Conference (HMC) or the Incorporated Association of Preparatory Schools (IAPS). Most independent schools were fundamentally on their own in what they were doing, and needed to be very clear just what this was.

Ten independent schools in Morrowshire and Robart were visited to discover the principles at the heart of their functioning and to see what effect the coexistence of maintained schools had on this *raison d'être*. The descriptions and pseudonyms of the schools are given below:

1. A boarding and day school for boys, aged 7–18, grouped in preparatory, junior and senior departments.   Waleyford Boys' School

2. Its associated girls' boarding and day school for ages 5–18 (preparatory and senior divisions).   Waleyford Girls' School

3. A 'famous' boys' boarding school for ages 13–18.   Hilliers

4. A progressive co-educational boarding and day School for ages 3–18.   Culinara School

5. A co-educational boarding and day school which follows particular philosophical principles.   Philosopher's School

6. A co-educational boarding and day school for children with a particular artistic gift.   Zenith School

7. A boys' day school for the secondary age group.   William Shakespeare

8. A girls' day school for ages 7–18.   Broadacre School

9. A boys' preparatory day school.   Mallory House

10. A co-educational preparatory day school.   Cadogan School

For several of the headteachers their school's *raison d'être* was a particular educational purpose. The headmaster of Mallory House, an IAPS preparatory school, saw himself as running a school which provided a particular kind of education, an education which was in itself an excellent grounding moving well into the secondary stage, but which also prepared boys to go on and complete their education at one of a number of boys's public schools, both day and boarding. For Mr Standish there *was* an independent educational 'system' in that there was, for boys, a recognisable pathway from type of school (preparatory) to type of school (public). He himself favoured boarding schools at this subsequent stage, though not during the preparatory stage. The appropriate rite of passage, following the education provided by his school, was Common Entrance. Boys at Mallory House were *not*, be said, prepared for the type of 'intelligence test' selection at age 11 through which some of the public schools admitted pupils before the Common Entrance intake at age 13. Any boy from Mallory House wanting to move on at 11 must 'take his chance' with such a test.

The preparatory school in its present-day form is a relatively recent creation (Leinster-Mackay 1984) compared with many of the public schools, but the *raison d'être* of Mallory House, as a school of this type which guided boys along a path which led to another well-established phase of education, can be described as a 'traditional' educational *raison d'être*.

Another school with an educational *raison d'être* was Cadogan. This was a co-educational school for boys and girls aged 2½ to 13. Unlike Mallory House which (like the majority of IAPS schools) had charitable status, Cadogan was run as a business.[2] It laid emphasis on a particular kind of teaching – formal, with an early introduction of subject specialisms, and the intention of taking every child beyond the norms of achievement for the age group. Whether children moved on at 11 or 13 was immaterial to Mr Norris, the headmaster, so far as his educational aims were concerned (although the leaving age did of course have implications for his general business planning and the overall structure of his school). If Cadogan had done its work with the child, he or she would be advantageously equipped to move either into a maintained or an independent secondary school; it was not, Mr Norris said, a matter of principle for him that one particular sector should receive his pupils. Wherever they went, they would be off to a good start. This could be described as a 'maximising' educational *raison d'être*.

All the secondary-stage independent schools which were exclusively for boys (Hilliers, William Shakespeare School and the senior department of Waleyford Boys' School) also emphasised an educational *raison d'être*. They did not, interestingly enough, claim that their 'all boys' population was a matter of principle, in itself justifying the existence of the school as an institution offering a particular educational benefit to the young male (although we shall see that some independent girls schools *did* seem to have such a gender-based *raison d'être*.) The three boys' schools stressed instead the style and focus of their teaching and that the boys who attended their schools must be to some extent academically capable of responding to such teaching.

In the case of Hilliers, the boys enrolled for its high calibre, costly, all-round education had in the past come mainly from successive generations of the same families (with an additional substantial contingent from overseas). The present headmaster claimed that this was no longer the case. Public school and boy pupil were now more carefully matched to each other, and family tradition was not an overriding reason for acceptance. This head-master was in fact denying the present-day existence of a class-based *raison d'être* for his school and was emphasising instead the education which the school provided, from which boys from a certain range of academic ability could best profit.

Despite certain differences between them, which were linked to their day or boarding character, the three senior boys' schools can all be described as having an 'academic' *raison d'être* which could be distinguished from the 'traditional' or 'maximising' educational *raisons d'être* of the preparatory schools described earlier.

In complete contrast to those schools which had as their central purpose the provision of a particular kind of education, was the school which had the *raison d'être* of meeting the needs of an unusual type of child. The Zenith School was for an élite, boys and girls who in the literal sense were 'chosen or elected ones', endowed with a particular artistic gift. The school adapted its curriculum, organisation and staffing to meet the individual needs of these gifted boys and girls. The headmaster saw the school as particularly able to encourage and develop the gifts of those who in an ordinary school environ-ment had found themselves ridiculed or criticised as inadequate, and who needed an environment in which their artistry could be the unquestioned centre of their life and endeavour.

Different again, in their *raisons d'être* were the two schools which purveyed an ethos rather than a particular form of education. Culinara was a Quaker school in its foundation. Its present-day practice emphasised self-government by the pupils and a particular health-orientated life-style for all within its influence. Culinara was an unusual and distinctive school, but could be classified with other long-standing progressive schools as one of a small and recognisable group of institutions (although these institutions were in no way affiliated to one another).

The Philosopher's School, on the other hand, defied classification. Only those familiar with the world-view of the seer, whose approach to life it perpetuated, could fully appreciate its ethos. The school had no headteacher and its policies were explained by one teacher on behalf of a group of those teachers recognised as fully committed members of the staff. He stressed that interested families must and did seek the school out. The staff took the view that children 'came towards the school – destiny plays a part in that'. Accepting a child into the school was perceived as a long-term commit-ment to that particular human being. 'To do any good, you really need to be a Philosopher's pupil from the word go', that is, from a young age. But the family too must be in sympathy with the aims of the school. 'If home and school are not as one, the school has to say "Goodbye" to the child'.

Both these schools recognised that they were likely to benefit the type of child who might be described as emotionally vulnerable, but this was seen as a by-product of their underlying reason for existence. Meeting the needs of such children was not in itself the *raison d'être* of either school.

The two girls' schools (Waleyford Girls' and Broadacre School) shared a *raison d'être* which was gender-based. If they ceased to be girls' schools, their existence as recognisable institutions would undoubtedly have been at an end. Providing an education for girls was what they were primarily and distinctively about, the one on a day-school basis for girls aged 7 to 18, the other educating girls from 5 to 18, with a boarding facility for girls over the age of 8. Both the schools provided a formal education of the academic type and were as far as possible selective of girls with some academic ability. However, the headmistresses of these schools recognised that that proportion of their pupils who came in at age 5 or age 7 could only be selected for general capacity, and no further entrance hurdles were placed before them at later stages of their life in the school (although the headmistress of Broadacre occasionally suggested to parents that their daughter might be happier, at the secondary stage, at a less academically orientated school).

All of these ten independent schools, then, had a recognisable *raison d'être*. In summary, one school existed to respond to the needs of individuals with a particular gift. Seven had as their *raisons d'être* the kind of education they purveyed, and two more were gender-orientated in their *raisons d'être*, in that they existed specifically to educate girls. The two other schools existed to purvey a particular approach to life.

What effect does the coexistence of maintained schools have on the raisons d'être of independent schools?

In considering the relevance of the maintained sector for independent schools, three main possibilities exist. Headteachers may see their schools as in competition with maintained schools offering a similar type of education, or claim to supplement the maintained sector by offering a form of education not available in local-authority schools. Alternatively, it is conceivable that the headteacher of an independent school may operate in a state of complete detachment from the maintained sector, drawing on a discrete set of pupils and seemingly unaware of the local authority and its education system.

None of the independent schools seemed to be operating totally without regard to the coexisting maintained schools. It would be difficult to imagine that any independent school could do so in the 1980s. If only for politically tactful reasons, independent schools could not afford to keep themselves totally to themselves as far as the existence of maintained education was concerned, and for a number of practical reasons they might need to acknowledge and indeed foster contacts with the maintained schools and the local authority. Even schools which had no wish to attract local-authority funding, and preferred to be unencumbered by any financial connection with the education committee, were unlikely to ignore totally the local authority and its schools. If they had charitable status, they might choose to emphasise that they were an asset to the community, ready to play a part in local life.

Those headteachers of independent schools who could look back over a number of years of their school's coexistence with the maintained sector had some foundation for making the claim that their school now played a complementary role *vis-à-vis* the maintained schools. They were providing a form of education which was no longer available in local authority schools. In the case of the Zenith School, the claim to a complementary role was even more clear-cut. An education responsive to particular artistic gifts had never been available within the maintained sector, and even the 1976 Education Act, which required local authorities to have regard to the general principle of secondary education, which was unselective by ability, had made an exception in the case of music and dancing, and authorised local education authorities to continue to fund places at fee-paying schools which educated children with these artistic gifts. So far as the Zenith School was concerned, the availability of some DES grants for pupils, and the continued funding of some pupils by their local authorities (although this practice was much reduced compared with past years) put the school clearly in a complementary role with the maintained sector, even though the great majority of their pupils' fees were paid for by their parents.

Several of the other schools could contend that they were rounding out educational provision in the area because they filled a gap left (they claimed) by an authority's former grammar schools. These schools (which included the Waleyford schools, Broadacre School and the William Shakespeare School) were not described by their headteachers as having, in former days, been in direct competition with such local-authority grammar schools. Rather, they spoke in terms of a formerly 'shared task' or 'having a great deal in common'. Most of the headteachers had spent part of their teaching career in the maintained sector, and the headteacher of the William Shakespeare School, Mr Ajax, had taught for many years in a local-authority grammar school. He considered that all his educational ideas had been acquired in the maintained sector, towards which he continued to have the warmest feelings. In common with some of the other independent school headteachers, he experienced some guilt about the relative easiness of his school's task, teaching a selected group of pupils on long-established and traditional lines, whereas colleagues in the comprehensive schools had to 'cope with every type of pupil, and pursue a wide range of aims.'

The headmistress of Waleyford Girls' had had her own education in the maintained sector and done her teaching practice there. Her subsequent teaching career in the independent sector had begun fortuitously. She too had an image of a former, closer relationship of her school with the local authority, but it was an impression of a school slightly apart from and above the local education system, to which the local authority formerly sent selected 'scholars'. Since the ending of the authority's own funding of assisted places, the school and the authority were more at a distance from one another, and any give and take of coexistence activities took place with individual schools.

Although there was no longer any funding by local authorities of places in any of the schools with an academic or gender-based *raison d'être* (with the exception of one 'boarding need' place at Waleyford Boys' School), three of the schools offered assisted places under the government scheme, covered by the 1980 Education Act. The scheme was of value to the schools, but these headteachers had mixed feelings about it since it did nothing to strengthen their relationship with local authorities. Nevertheless, the basis of the scheme, with its implied accolade that there was something of 'benefit' to be gained by access to an independent education, gave governmental backing to the schools' claim of complementing what was available in the maintained sector. It also, however, gave a hostage to fortune in the event of a subsequent change of government, and the headteachers were conscious of this.

The two schools whose ethos was their *raison d'être* (Culinara and the Philosopher's School) were clearly in a position to claim complementarity to the maintained sector. In 1984 no less than sixteen local education authorities were funding one or more pupil's attendance at Culinara, which was used for pupils either with boarding need or special educational need for a nurturing environment. Culinara was not a special school, and since the 1981 Act the placement of any 'statemented' pupil there had to be individually approved by the secretary of state. The majority of pupils at the school were funded by parents who were willing and able to pay for what the school provided. Nevertheless, the school's intake of former maintained-sector pupils, paid for by their local authorities, was sufficient to justify Mr Harman, the headteacher of Culinara, in sending a circular letter to chief education officers updating them on what the school had to offer in 1984. But although Culinara obviously provided something not available in the maintained sector, he felt the school in fact had much more in common with the maintained sector than with other forms of independent education. Along with certain other 'progressive' schools, Culinara had been founded as a fully co-educational school with no corporal punishment and a child-centred outlook, with creative activities emphasised. These ideas, first treated with suspicion had, Mr Harman claimed, now been widely accepted in the state sector. Culinara was, by the 1980s, more distanced from other independent schools than from the maintained sector. This had some implications for survival strategies, which will be later discussed.

The Philosopher's School too always had a number of pupils who were paid for by local authorities. Not all the pupils proposed by local authorities were accepted, but all were interviewed, and this, the spokesman teacher contended, allowed the 'element of destiny' (which brought pupils to the school) 'to have sway'. Despite its idiosyncratic organisation and practices, the school did not hold itself totally aloof from all expectations and requirements of external educationalists. HMI visited the school from time to time and teachers found it was possible to convince HMI up to a point about the aims and objectives of the school, but 'then you had to part company and agree to differ on certain matters'. The school no longer had its own boarding houses, and pupils who did not live locally were boarded out with selected families in the area. Of the 5 per cent of pupils whose places at the school were funded by local authorities, at least half had a boarding need, and the school had to satisfy the local authorities concerned that its boarding arrangements were suitable. The Philosopher's School was even more detached than was Culinara from other schools in the private sector and had no links with the private-sector infrastructure. However, the spokesman stressed that the school was similarly detached from the maintained sector. The school should be seen as standing on its own, with a dedication to the principles on which it was based: 'The children need to come to us.'

The only headteacher of an independent school who clearly acknowledged a competitive relationship with other schools was Mr Norris of Cadogan. This preparatory school had only been under his ownership and leadership for a few years, and it was an expanding educational enterprise. The competition he offered was chiefly to other independent schools educating a similar age group. By having a slightly lower age of intake, and organising for pupil departures at either 11 or 13, Cadogan could cater for parents who did not want their child to have several changes of school during the early years.

So far as competition with the maintained sector was concerned, the headmaster saw Cadogan as offering an expert level of teaching, with specialisation at an earlier age than in the maintained sector and more rapid individual progress than pupils would achieve in the maintained primary schools. There was no shortage of parents prepared to pay for these advantages. The presence of his school might mean some children did not enter the maintained sector. But in an area where there was still an influx of young families this filtering-off could be defined as 'making room' in the maintained schools for families which were not yet financially 'ready' to consider the independent sector. Like several other independent headteachers, Mr Norris perceived fee-paying for education as a question of family priorities rather than spare resources, although he acknowledged that a certain level of financial stability had to be reached before such alternative priorities could be examined.

Cadogan school had not yet been asked to accept any pupils funded by a local authority, but Mr Norris did not rule this out. He was educating several children who had special educational needs, which were not as yet 'statemented'. He had an intimate knowledge of the workings and requirements of maintained education, having worked in it for a number of years and attended many courses at the DES. None of his teachers was a probationer, so all had had experience in maintained schools. Cadogan was, he considered, well able to meet any requirements which special-services education officers might have, in placing a child with special educational need. Local-authority advisers were well known to Mr Norris, and the authority could always be turned to for information and advice. However, the school was run as a business. It did not have charitable status, and this relieved the headmaster of any anxiety about possible political threats to such status.

These headteacher viewpoints make it clear that the *raison d'être* of an independent school, and the headteacher's approach to educational coexistence are interactive. The more unusual the *raison d'être* of the school, the easier it becomes to define coexistence as a state of complementarity rather than competition. But the existence of the maintained sector – and in particular any acceptance of funding or subsidy from local education authorities, rating authorities or central government – can have some effect on the *raison d'être* of a school, as when, for example, schools like Culinara or the Philosopher's School put themselves in some danger of becoming seen as 'special schools'.

Something else which influences the place taken by any independent school in the whole panoply of public and private education is the need for strategies for survival. In a time of falling rolls and economic constraint this need is shared with maintained-sector schools. A school's need to survive is quite distinct from its reason for existence. For any school to *continue* in existence three survival tasks must be continually tackled: ensuring a supply of pupils; acquiring and managing the services of teachers; acquiring and managing physical and financial resources. In the independent sector all of these tasks had to be addressed by the headteacher on behalf of the school. In some cases, but by no means in all the types of independent schools, these tasks were shared with a governing body and a bursar. But some aspects of all three groups of survival tasks were the direct concern of the headteacher of each independent school in a way which clearly distinguished the role from that of a headteacher in the maintained sector.[3]

To the observer it was evident that the three ever-present tasks were interactive with the *raison d'être* of the school. Patterns of coexistence were also influenced by survival tasks. The school's attitude to the coexistence of the maintained sector was not just a question of what the school was set up to do, compared with the maintained sector. It was also a question of what difficulties, or what advantages, the headteacher was experiencing in the performance of the three survival tasks, which affected relations and contacts with the maintained schools and also with other independent schools. The first priority and essential requirement of all schools was to ensure a supply of pupils, and this is examined in the next chapter.

FIVE

The Supply of Pupils to Independent and Maintained Schools

Earlier discussion of how education authorities assess likely pupil numbers made it plain that by no means all children of compulsory school age or rising 5 automatically find a place on the roll of their local primary school. Even at this early stage, the wishes of the parents play a part, although only a nominal part in some isolated areas where there are few accessible schools. It is the parent's task to approach the school in the first instance and ask for the child's name to be included in the appropriate year of intake. If the child is not registered with any maintained or aided school, that child, as a statistic of 'live births' but not as an individual, is presumed by the local authority to have enrolled at an independent school. Only if a known child disappears in mysterious circumstances – perhaps from the roll of a maintained nursery school – is the child's non-appearance in a local primary school likely to be followed up individually by the education welfare service.

If the parents do decide on a private education for their child, they immediately come up against an important difference between the maintained and independent sectors. All independent-sector schools are selective in the sense that they admit individuals, while maintained schools admit chiefly by age cohort. It is the date of birth of the child which makes possible the child's first entry to one or other of the authority's primary schools in the child's area of residence, and as long as the family remain in local residence, the child retains the right of entry to a free place in one of the authority's schools appropriate to his or her age group right through to the age of 16. This is the meaning of compulsory free education in a society and is one reason why independent schools have cause to be grateful for the coexistence of the maintained sector. It is always there, as a fall back, to meet statutory requirements for the compulsory schooling of any child they choose not to accept or retain. There is no similar fall back arrangement which the maintained schools can count on.[1]

But because the maintained sector is always there, and is free in the sense of not charging fees, independent schools which do charge fees need to adopt a more positive strategy to ensure a supply of pupils than maintained schools must undertake. However, the independent schools' task is made easier by one important characteristic. The independent sector is small. It has, at least hitherto, shown no corporate ambition to educate more than a minority of the school-age population, and the individual independent schools are characteristically also small. Most of the secondary schools are no bigger than a sizable primary school in the maintained sector, and the preparatory schools are likely to have no more than a couple of hundred pupils at most. The small size of the institution as a whole, as well as the (possible but not invariable) small size of each class, is felt to be valued by parents.[2] The schools are therefore organised to be viable with a small overall pupil population, and the 'supply of pupils' task is all the more readily completed.

Once having admitted a fee-paying pupil, however, the contract between school and parent is renewable every term, and there is always the possibility that for one reason or another the pupil will leave again. Mr Norris of Cadogan School had lowered his first age of intake to 2½ specifically in the hope that, having got the child installed at the nursery stage, the parents would think it preferable not to unsettle the child by making a move to another pre-prep school at the age of 3 or 4.

The independent schools visited in Morrowshire and Robart typically covered a much wider age range than any maintained primary or secondary school.[3] For a school which admitted pupils at age 5, 7, at 11-plus and at 16, exercising some form of selectivity at each stage, and where pupil admissions were not delegated to semi-autonomous junior and senior departments, the headteacher's role in selecting and admitting pupils was potentially considerable. Miss Cousins, the headteacher of Waleyford Girls' School, for example, was substantially involved in the admission of each and every child. Obviously, it would be helpful to headteachers if the expectation could be imparted to parents that children who once gained a place at the school did not typically leave again. But with ever-rising fees, no absolute requirement of this kind could be made. In any case, most of the independent-school headteachers considered some pupil departures to be inevitable, because fee-paying parents were likely to be mobile in their careers.

Family mobility was, however, a fact of life for headteachers of maintained as well as independent schools, throughout the geographical area of Robart and Morrowshire. But maintained schools had to accept unexpected arrivals as well as departures. In a time of falling rolls, such arrivals were generally welcomed in the maintained schools. Nevertheless, in an authority like Robart, where for some years 30 per cent of all live births had been to mothers born outside the United Kingdom, ethnic-minority groups were substantial and among the most mobile. Unexpected additions to maintained-school rolls during the school year were often of pupils whose mother tongue was not English. Such arrivals made an unpredictable demand on limited resources.

Pupil movement between the sectors

Maintained schools did not span the same wide age range of children as the independent schools, and this fact had an influence on headteacher attitudes to pupil departures to the independent sector. The relatively shorter time during which each maintained institution had to retain its pupils (typically from 5 to 7 or 8 in first or infants schools, from 7 to 11 or from 8 to 12 in middle schools and from 11 or 12 to 16 in secondary schools)[4] meant that any movement of pupils from the maintained sector was not usually a direct loss to any headteacher. Such movement was likely to take place between educational stages. Although the non-arrival of a pupil did deplete the roll of the next-stage school, the headteacher of that school could do nothing about it. In education authorities where the long-established coexistence of well thought of independent schools made some intersectoral mobility of pupils seem inevitable and acceptable, it was not surprising that the departure of pupils to the independent sector at the end of an educational stage was readily accepted if not positively fostered by some maintained-school headteachers. The regular movement of pupils from a maintained, infant, junior or middle school to independent preparatory or secondary schools was in some cases seen by interested prospective parents as a feather in the maintained school's cap. Headteachers had their own personal views on the desirability of private schooling and on the choice of an independent school for a particular pupil's next stage of education, but appeared to adhere strictly to the professional position that this was a matter for the parent's decision. There were, however, circumstances in which the movement of pupils from the maintained to the independent sector was not a neutral matter of no immediate concern to the maintained-school headteacher. Two examples can be given.

In one Morrowshire village school the notion of a geographically based and community-related catchment area for pupils was evidently an experienced reality for the headteacher of the school. Local education authority policy that catchment areas were not used as criteria for pupil admission, at either the primary or the secondary stage – and central-government policy that parents should have freedom of choice not only between schools but also across local-authority borders – might have to be formally acknowledged but were not the stuff of everyday life. The headteacher of this small junior mixed and infants' village school was active in the local community and appeared able to exercise face-to-face social control over parents of local children. The intake to his school fluctuated by as much as 50 per cent from one year to the next because of overall demographic change. He accepted this as inevitable and also accepted that a certain percentage of local children were always educated in the private sector and a further percentage would move into it at secondary stage. But he was not prepared to accept that children should start at his school at the age of 5, then move off to a preparatory school after he and his teaching staff had done all the groundwork on them. He claimed to minimise this by counselling parents directly that if pupils started at the school, they should remain there at least until the age of 10. If the intention was to use the independent sector from age 7, another school accepting 5-year-olds should be found for the child. Such direct management of parental choice would probably only be effective in a small community, but some degree of headteacher influence is always likely to temper parental choice and pupil movement, whatever local and central government policies may be.

Another example where pupil movement to the private sector was a matter of direct concern for the headteachers of maintained schools occurred in Robart, where the secondary age of transfer, at 12, did not coincide with the admission of 11-year-olds to local independent secondary schools. Ever since the middle- and high-school system had been set up in 1973, certain middle schools had regularly lost between 20 and 50 per cent of their final-year pupils to the private sector at age 11. This had become a fact of life for the schools, and indeed the evidence that these middle schools were for some a staging post en route to an independent school was one of several reasons for their popularity. However, falling pupil numbers and financial constraints in the authority as a whole were heightening the importance of the 'numbers game' for individual schools. Robart, like many other education authorities, strove to avoid school closure by artificially restricting admissions to its more popular middle schools to the same numbers as other schools. Resources were allocated to the schools on the basis of pupil numbers, so when many pupils moved off early from a popular middle school, joining the independent sector, the middle school's staffing and other resources for its final-year pupils were accordingly reduced. At one such school, teacher attitudes to educational coexistence were undoubtedly influenced by this 'knock on' effect of pupil departures. The headteacher found it necessary to stress to staff the professional attitude of leaving parents free to decide what was in the best interest of their child.

The transmission of information about pupils from maintained schools to independent schools was no small task, especially for the heads of junior schools where a proportion of pupils sat numerous entrance exams for independent secondary schools. The headteacher of a primary school in Robart received letters from the heads of thirteen different independent schools, over a four-month period (November 1983 to January 1984). The letters asked for varying forms of information about eighteen pupils in all, who had applied for places at the schools concerned.[5] Some of the independent-school headteachers supplied report forms to be filled in. One approach was highly conciliatory and tactful; others verged on the peremptory. One letter asked how several applicants compared in academic merit; another, for the results of any standardised tests. Some headteachers were interested to hear of any family or health problems, while one independent head evidently used the same *pro forma* letter in correspondence with maintained heads as he did with any independent-sector colleagues and was chiefly concerned to learn whether the parents concerned had 'met, up to date, all their obligations' to the child's present school. All the communications gave short deadlines for reply. The primary-school headteacher had in fact designed a *pro forma* of his own, as had the headteacher of another primary school in Robart who was also inundated with requests for information from independent-school heads. They found it too time-consuming for them and their staff to prepare replies adapted to the requests of the particular independent school. There was a particular reluctance to compare the academic merits of classmates who were seeking entry to the same school.

Choosing pupils

Although for popular maintained schools local-authority policy about the management of pupil admissions might have its disadvantages, for the most part its effect was to relieve maintained schools' headteachers of major responsibility for the survival task of ensuring a supply of pupils. Through open days, open evenings, informative documents and home/school relations, headteacher and staff might do what they could to encourage parents to enrol children at the school, but the full weight of concern about coping with demographic change in the compulsory school-age population fell not on the school but on the local authority.

Equally, the authorities' policy of comprehensive or all-ability secondary education meant that heads of maintained schools were not involved in pupil selection, as were the heads of independent schools. For example, two single-sex high schools in Robart were regularly oversubscribed by parental preference, and pupil names were selected by a computerised random-selection procedure carried out in the education department of the authority. The headteachers of the single-sex high schools confirmed that they, like the headteachers of other maintained high schools in Robart, had no say whatever in the allocation of places to 12-year-olds at their schools.

Parental preference had by law to be taken account of each time pupils were transferred to a new stage of education at a different school, but the terms of the 1980 Education Act enabled authorities to 'manage' parental preference in line with their own policies.[6] Appeals procedures, also provided for in the 1980 Act, might override authority allocation from time to time, and this was not always to the displeasure of headteachers of popular but artificially restricted maintained schools. Nevertheless, it was parent rather than headteacher preference for the admission of a particular pupil which occasioned the appeal. Transfers of pupils at later stages of secondary schooling were more within headteachers' remit, and practice varied in the admission monitoring which took place. The headmistress of the girls' high school, for example, still left the matter entirely in the hands of the local authority, while at the boys' school the headmaster usually interviewed parents and would-be entrants at age 13 and upwards, passing on his views to the education office.

In the independent schools, by contrast, selection procedures were a regular part of school life. Almost all the schools claimed that although there might be casual vacancies in the pupil population from time to time when someone had moved away, at the formal intake stages every vacancy was sought after, usually by from two to three applicants at the younger ages. For some schools at the secondary stage there were as many as four applicants for each place. The criteria of selection at the early ages were by no means exclusively academic. Mr Standish of Mallory House saw his long-established preparatory school as an institution active in the local community, to which the whole family of the pupil, not just the pupil himself, could become committed. The attitude of the parents was paramount in his yearly selection of an intake of twenty-five boys. 'Basically, if I like the parent, I will have the child. I have got to work with those parents for nine years. If I dislike the parents, even if the boy is bright I wouldn't have him'. When children came in at 4 they were not tested. Once the school had taken a child, if the parents were supportive and the child was happy, he would keep him.

The headteachers who accepted young pupils all agreed that children could not be selected for academic ability at 5 years or under. For some, including Mr Norris of Cadogan, this meant that logically there should not be academic selection of children coming in at a later age. Others, however, appeared to make a formal assessment of the ability of all applicants for places at age 7 or thereafter, confirming the local opinion that it was easier to get into the schools at the earliest age of intake than it would be later on.

At the secondary stage, stringent combinations of academic testing and formal interview played a part in an annual-intake selection process which made heavy demands on the headteacher and senior staff of an independent school. For example, at the William Shakespeare School there might be 280 applicants for the sixty-six places available at age 11. If eighty were weeded out by the entrance exam as academically unable to benefit, 200 boys and their parents remained to be interviewed. On the basis of these interviews, and any reports supplied by the boy's previous schools, Mr Ajax, the headteacher of William Shakespeare School, had to make the 'policy decision of which boys are wanted in the school'. The lengthy interview programme was followed because Mr Ajax considered that somewhere at the bottom of the acceptable exam mark range he might find 'a nugget of gold', in the shape of a boy with particular musical, artistic or sporting gifts, or certain qualities of temperament. As soon as the 11-plus interviewing was completed each year, the

13-plus interviewing had to begin. This was for the twelve to fifteen boys admitted from preparatory school, having taken the Common Entrance exam. Holding certain places for an intake at age 13 was in line with traditional practice in independent education. But among those boys seeking entrance at 11, Mr Ajax frequently selected boys formerly at maintained schools, who had not been so intensively coached for the entrance exam as independent sector pupils were liable to be. A 'warts and all' assessment was, he considered, more possible when applicants came from maintained schools.

With the steady flow of applications for entry to each intake stage, the William Shakespeare School did not feel the competition of the maintained sector during the compulsory school years. There was, however, direct competition with other independent schools within a 10- to 15-mile radius, seeking to recruit the same type of academic boy. The headmasters of a group of these well thought of schools, including Mr Ajax, synchronised their offers of places, following the hectic period of entrance exams and interviews of 11-year-old applicants each year, so that parents would know on the same day where their son stood with regard to the various schools whose exams he had sat. This informal co-operation about the offer of places, re-established at a meeting each year of the headteachers concerned, was to ensure that the schools did not 'poach' from each other's lists. One of them had a number of academic scholarships to distribute, while William Shakespeare School had markedly fewer. It was right that parents should be able to decide which place to accept, in full knowledge of what the financial and other implications would be at each school. The annual meeting of headteachers also encouraged them to keep each other informed about the level of fees, the dates of open days, and generally to act as a reference group of colleagues.

However, the headmaster of William Shakespeare saw some disadvantages in the arrangement, from the point of view of the prospective pupils. It meant that a boy whose parents wanted him to have a chance with all the schools concerned had to do exam after exam, and interview after interview, perhaps ending up with six offers of a school place, on the same day in March. He favoured the idea of the schools operating a joint entrance-exam system, with applicants naming a first, second and third choice on their original application. But some of his fellow headmasters were opposed to this idea on the grounds that their valued 'independence' would cease to be total.

Although independent secondary schools might welcome applications from pupils whose primary education had been in the maintained sector, they did not typically use fee reductions or scholarships restricted to maintained-sector pupils as part of any strategy for keeping up the pupil numbers. Hilliers had one such scholarship in its gift for a comprehensive schoolboy of 16 who exhibited leadership qualities, but the headmaster considered it would be politically and professionally tactless, in the 1980s, to pursue the recruitment of such a boy on a scholarship basis. Waleyford Boys' School had two partial scholarships for pupils from local middle schools in the maintained sector. These scholarships had been endowed before the 1980 introduction of the assisted-places scheme.

The offer of assisted places

Schools offering assisted places (of which the two Waleyford schools and the William Shakespeare School were examples), did so through a participation agreement with the DES. The scheme had the advantage (in terms of the peaceful coexistence of these schools with the local education authority) that the assisted-place schools were not seen to be recruiting from the maintained schools of any particular local authority but rather from the maintained sector generally.

Schools had differing policies about the stage at which the availability of an assisted place became part of the admission procedure. At Waleyford Girls' School, for example, six assisted places were available at age 11. Girls from maintained primary schools or middle schools had to satisfy normal entry requirements, but in seeking an assisted place they competed only with each other, not with the whole group of girls seeking fee-paying entry at age 11. But at the William Shakespeare School all applicants sat the entrance exam and were placed in a ranked order of merit. After interviewing was completed, Mr Ajax drew up his final list of boys to be offered places at the school, and only then combed through to see which boys among them were likely to be eligible for one of the available assisted places. He did not wish the scheme to influence his judgment of who should rightly be admitted to the school, and perceived some other schools as 'giving away assisted places like confetti' to people who would otherwise never have got in.

For the bursar of the Waleyford schools, the administration of the scheme was a welcomed but nevertheless burdensome administrative task. Estimates had to be prepared each year of the amount of tuition income which would be required from the DES for each place, and what extra income would be needed for examination fees, lunches, uniform, travel, and so on. Any subsequent fee increases had to be notified to the DES within a statutory period, otherwise these would not be payable by the DES. The schools received the assisted-place money in proportions of one-third each school term. In the case of a pupil with an assisted place, a normal bill for tuition and other costs was sent to the parent with the amount payable by the DES shown as a credit. Only in a very few cases would there be nothing further for the parents to pay.

One of the most difficult balancing acts for all the schools offering assisted places appeared to be the maintenance of the required 60:40 ratio of places awarded to pupils formerly at maintained and fee-paying schools, respectively. A pupil had to have been at a maintained school for at least two years to be eligible for inclusion in the 60 per cent 'maintained school' proportion. But a pupil who had been in fee-paying education for no more than two terms, prior to application for an assisted place, had to be included among the 40 per cent of 'formerly fee-paying' recipients. Yet, as Mr Raikes of Waleyford Boys' School pointed out, the independent schools were far more likely to be able to identify pupils from among their own populations whose family circumstances might entitle them to an assisted place. Families with children formerly in the maintained sector had to take the initiative in approaching the school and making a case for their child's eligibility for an assisted place. Schools knew nothing about the families concerned and sometimes felt it politic to make enquiries through a third party in case parents were misrepresenting their circumstances. In the delicate political climate regarding the independent schools in the 1980s, Mr Ajax of William Shakespeare, among others, recognised that the schools could not risk being accused of maladministration of the scheme. One way and another, the 60:40 balance was difficult to achieve, and if sufficient suitable applicants could not be found on the 'formerly maintained' side, this further reduced the number of places available on the 'formerly fee-paying' side. However, the participating schools acknowledged that the intention of the scheme was not to help the child who was having difficulty in continuing in independent schooling for financial reasons. It was unequivocally to enable children who had previously been educated in the maintained sector to take up a place at an independent school.

The 16-plus age group

The whole question of 16-plus education in terms both of the sources of a supply of pupils and of appropriate institutional arrangements, was a pressing educational concern for headteachers and principals in both the independent and maintained sectors.[7] The movement of pupils at 16-plus was a noticeable feature of education in Morrowshire and Robart. There was a general impression that more pupils were moving from independent to maintained-sector institutions at that stage than were transferring in the reverse direction, but the facts were far from clearly established. Pupil movement at the 16-plus stage also took place *within* each sector. As one headteacher put it, '16-plus has become a watershed of change. At one time pupils who were going on to sixth-form studies expected to do so in their present secondary school.' That expectation no longer prevailed.

Morrowshire and Robart had different arrangements for 16-plus education. In the smaller authority, high-school pupils wishing to continue their secondary schooling normally did so in one of the authority's three sixth-form colleges. A minority of 16-year-olds sought a place in the Robart College of Further Education. The policy decision had already been taken to reorganise all the institutions concerned into three tertiary colleges, but this plan would not be implemented until the late 1980s. In Morrowshire, on the other hand, all the secondary schools covered the 11 to 18 age range. There were also nine further-education colleges in the county. Maintaining the viability of all the secondary schools and colleges where 16-plus pupils could currently be educated was an unresolved educational policy problem in Morrowshire, and one about which some headteachers appeared more concerned than others.

One of the 11-to-18 comprehensives was a popular school oversubscribed by parental preference for the 158 places which, under county policy, comprised its agreed intake at 11-plus. At 16-plus the school typically had on roll a total sixth-form (covering two year-groups) of over 200 pupils, but the number was falling gradually, and the headmaster expected this trend to continue. During the three academic years from 1981 to 1983, the intake of pupils to the sixth form came from the sources shown in Table 2.

The figures in Table 2 were supplied by the headteacher. They show that in 1982 and 1983 approximately 30 per cent of the intake to the first-year sixth form did not stay on for a second year of sixth-form studies. They also show that for three years the intake to the sixth form from other maintained schools was greater than the intake from independent schools. But the head was critical of some of his colleagues in other local-authority schools who never seemed to look beyond their own boundaries to see what range of independent schools served the same age groups as themselves. He himself was alert to a number of developments in local independent schools which he anticipated might influence pupil movement between the sectors at 16-plus over the next few years. In the view of this headteacher in the maintained sector, schools should put the best interests of the pupils before any question of maintaining a viable sixth-form size at a time of demographic decline and economic difficulty. Honesty of advice was all-important, and fifth formers should not be encouraged to come back to the school in the sixth form if it would be more in their interests to look for a job or some form of training.

While the headteacher of an 'all through' secondary school might be able to

Table 2 Sources of sixth-form-pupil intake, 1981–83

Source of pupil	1981	1982	1983
Fifth year of the school	91	105	97
Other maintained or voluntary-aided schools	12	21*	11
Independent schools	7	9	5
Pupils from overseas	3	1	—
	113	136	113
On roll of second-year sixth form	104	80	90
Total on roll of sixth form	217	216	203

* This figure was boosted by the closure of one local school.

contemplate with some degree of equanimity the possibility of decline in his sixth-form roll, in the case of a sixth-form college which catered *only* for the 16-to-18 age group, ensuring a supply of such pupils was a task quite different from that addressed by institutions handling the compulsory school-age range. Pupils of 16 and over are not required by law to continue their schooling. Pupils of compulsory school age at independent schools, or at oversubscribed schools in the maintained sector, might all be on the roll by virtue of a positive choice of a particular institution, but they would in any case all have to go to school somewhere. Pupils at the 16-plus stage are not in that position, and for maintained-sector institutions dealing exclusively with that age group, this brings an entirely new element into pupil admissions. The sixth-form college has to sell itself to pupils and parents even though it does not charge fees. Opportunity costs (to the pupils who might be occupying their time in some other way) are in question. If the college succeeds in its selling so well that it is oversubscribed, it has to embark on a selection and admission programme which at least equals in complexity the programme followed by independent secondary schools. There is the added complication that the sixth-form college, if part of a local-authority's system of comprehensive education, should not be seen as becoming an élitist institution.

The extent of influx from the private schools to Robart's sixth-form colleges was a fairly closely monitored phenomenon, but the large colleges of further and higher education did not collate the information which they held about students' previous place of schooling. As the principal of one of the colleges pointed out, since the information on enrolment cards was not yet fed into computer files, the college did not know what markets they were addressing. Entrepreneurial activity was based on impressionistic discussions with heads of departments about enrolment trends.[8]

When the question of 16-plus education was raised with headteachers of the independent schools, almost all the heads of schools which had sixth forms agreed that there was a distinctive shift in their pupil population at this stage. The exception was the head of Hilliers. Any wish which boys might have to go somewhere else at age 16 was inhibited, he considered, by the thought that such early departure from a famous school would always be seen as suspect by future assessors of the individual's *curriculum vitae*. But at both the Waleyford schools, at Broadacre and at William Shakespeare, headteachers found that sixth-form sizes and the individuals who would make up the sixth form were becoming unpredictable. Girls left from the girls' schools; boys left from the boys' schools. None of these schools was organised to accept pupils of the opposite sex into their sixth forms. Waleyford Boys' School might have liked to do so, but a suggested amalgamation with Waleyford Girls' had been fiercely resisted by the girls' school a few years earlier. And as the headmistress of Broadacre pointed out, while it might be fashionable for girls to move to boys' schools at 16-plus, there was no sign of it becoming fashionable for boys to join the sixth form of girls' schools. Most of the unexpected departures of potential sixth formers from both boys' and girls' schools were perceived as being not to other independent schools but to the maintained sector. For the headteachers concerned it meant that some pupils for a variety of reasons were choosing not to reap the benefit of what was perceived as the best these schools had to give, the culminating years of the academic and, in the case of the girls' schools, gender-related education which was their *raison d'être*.

Although the numbers concerned were not large, and the schools' sixth forms were by no means decimated, the implications of the phenomenon of pupil departure at 16 were of fundamental concern for the schools. In the maintained sector some local education authorities, like Robart, had long since acknowledged the logistical need to group a dwindling sixth-form population in separate institutions (and by doing so had tapped an additional supply of pupils prepared to move from the private sector at that stage). Other authorities, like Morrowshire, were moving inexorably towards the point where something radical would have to be done to preserve the viability of 16-plus education. The consortia into which clusters of schools had been nominally grouped with a college of further education had not become an administrative or educational reality, and the sixth forms of some schools were sinking below a workable size.

If, like the maintained sector, the independent sector were also to have to reorganise itself so as to provide separate institutions for 16- to 18-year-olds, this would strike at the heart of what many of these independent schools stood for. Moreover, such institutions might not prove successful. Many parents and pupils in the private sector might have been supporting the sixth form of their school out of loyalty, simply because it *was* their school. If faced with a move to another fee-paying institution, the choice between this and the maintained-sector institution would be more clear-cut and freed from 'old school' sentiment or sense of commitment. Moreover, the assumption which many maintained-sector headteachers made, but which few independent headteachers were prepared to support, that parents chose the independent sector during the compulsory school years to keep their offspring away from the unselected mass of school-age pupils, might prove to be correct.

Maintained-school pupils who went on to maintained-sector sixth-form colleges were self-selected as individuals, or members of families, who saw a value in continuing their education. The colleges already were seen as an acceptable setting for the sixth-form education of some ex-independent school pupils. If independent education at 16-plus were to be reorganised into separate institutions, very many more families might conclude that a maintained-sector college would be both acceptable and cheaper.

The question of ensuring a supply of pupils (in either sector) at 16-plus is however even more complicated than it has already been shown to be. In Robart, and in many other education authorities throughout the country, post-compulsory education was in the throes of being reorganised yet again. Sixth-form colleges were to become tertiary colleges, bringing under one roof a far wider range of courses, and also of maturity and type of student. The advantages and disadvantages of such a metamorphosis had been debated in theory but not yet experienced in practice. In particular it was not yet clear how parents of 16-year-olds would evaluate the social and educational qualities of the colleges. The tertiary colleges would perhaps increase the popularity of 16-plus education and also draw a larger number of pupils from the independent sector. On the other hand, the change to tertiary colleges might dry up the supply of students from the independent sector and send a reverse flow from the maintained high schools to fee-paying education for two years. Educational coexistence, and what it meant in terms of ensuring a supply of pupils, was by no means a cut-and-dried situation in the 1980s, any more than at any other time.

SIX

Managing Resources in the Independent School

We have seen that many, often unpredictable, factors influenced the supply of pupils to independent and maintained schools. Because of the relative buoyancy of the independent sector in the early 1980s, independent-school heads directed their energies to controlling the flow of pupils by various forms of selection, but might have been at a loss as to how to stimulate an increase had the supply showed signs of drying up.

The other essentials for the survival of a school – teaching staff and financial resources – presented a further set of management tasks for headteachers of independent schools. The approach they were able to take, and how it compared with the situation in the maintained sector, is examined in this chapter.

Teaching staff

New recruits to the teaching profession who wish to teach in maintained schools must have a teaching qualification and must serve a probationary period in a local-authority school during which their performance is appraised with the help of local-authority advisers.

Independent schools make their own decisions about the qualifications of staff. Probably a higher proportion of teachers in the independent sector are graduates, compared with the maintained sector, but a smaller proportion have degrees or certificates which constitute a formal teaching qualification. The many teachers in independent schools who do have such certification gained it in publicly funded colleges, and in many cases did their teaching practice in maintained or aided schools, but may have had their own schooling in the independent sector. A certificated teacher cannot serve a recognised probationary period in an independent school since local-authority advisers have no jurisdiction in such schools.

During 1984 and 1985, the *Times Educational Supplement* (*TES*) regularly carried between three and five pages of advertisements for teaching posts, including headteacher posts, in independent schools. One of the headteachers defined this as a relatively recent development, indicating that independent and maintained schools were fishing the same pool for teachers. Readership surveys carried out for the *TES* in 1977 and 1984 appear to support this analysis. In both years the *TES* was read by around 50 per cent of all school teachers. But the readership of independent school teachers had decreased from 53 per cent in 1977 to 34 per cent in 1984. If advertisers of independent-school posts in the *TES* are aware of this shift in readership, it must be presumed that they are at least as interested in recruiting maintained-school teachers as they are in teachers already working in independent schools.

With regard to possible teacher movement out of the independent sector, in search of senior management roles or headships in the maintained sector, independent heads considered such movement increasingly unlikely, particularly in the secondary schools. Now that most maintained secondary education was on comprehensive lines, while the majority of independent secondary schools remained academically selective, it was debatable whether teachers in either sector had the relevant experience to move up 'on the other side'. Teachers in the independent sector had experience of teaching the very able, an experience which should still be of use to them in the maintained sector, but might not be seen as compensating for the fact that they did not have extensive experience of remedial pupils or ethnic minorities.[1] In the reverse direction, if a teacher from the maintained sector was considered for a leadership post such as head of department in an independent school, the question of the ideas and assumptions which the teacher might bring from the other sector would be strongly in the independent head's mind.

During the period of the research, many actual headships of independent schools were widely advertised. When the eventual appointments were announced, the impression was gained that upwardly mobile headteachers in the independent schools were playing musical chairs within the sector. And although some of the headteachers in the independent schools contacted had at one time worked in the maintained sector, they had usually been appointed as heads after they had already moved over to the independent sector in a less senior capacity.

Teachers' pay and conditions of service in independent schools

The enquiries made in Morrowshire and Robart did not enable a detailed comparison of rates of pay in the maintained and independent schools. The headmistress of Broadacre said that in every respect her school was like a local-authority school so far as the teaching staff were concerned. Their conditions of service were identical to what they would have in a maintained school. Most of the independent-school headteachers said that teachers salaries were 'Burnham-related'. As a general rule, teachers might receive salaries slightly above the Burnham rate, but not markedly so. The main reason for maintaining a pay structure which was not straightforwardly the Burnham scale was that the school was not obliged automatically to adjust its salaries when increases in the Burnham rate were agreed. A proportional increase would normally be made in the salaries of teachers at the independent school, but this need not occur on the same date as the Burnham-agreed change.

Most of the schools appeared to have a flood of applications for every teaching post. Mr Norris of Cadogan employed only qualified teachers, many of them on a part-time basis. He claimed that 'in an area like this, teachers are queueing up to work at the school'. Some parents contacted in the research had the impression that certain key teachers at long-established independent schools were exceptionally highly paid, but no confirmation was provided for this belief.

Teachers working with boarding pupils had some additional rewards. These would, an officer of the Independent Schools' Bursars Association (ISBA) suggested, be likely to be a couple of points of increment within a scale rather than the award of a higher-scale post. Some of the rewards of boarding-school work were 'in kind'. As the bursar of the two Waleyford schools pointed out, housemasters or housetutors usually have the 'run of their teeth', (i.e. free food) and their accommodation, and this was deemed to be a remuneration for their extra duties. These perquisites were taxable. The headmaster of Hilliers contended that teachers in maintained boarding schools would be eligible for specific 'boarding extras' payments, which residential teachers at his famous school did not receive.

About 90 per cent of the independent secondary schools affiliated to ISBA paid the straight Burnham scale. However, the distribution of posts was a matter for the school itself. Teachers who are paid at the Burnham rate, in independent as well as maintained schools, must belong to the DES pension scheme. So long as the schools made the employer's contribution, in respect of the pension scheme, the DES would not question the overall salary structure of the independent school. This meant that the schools were not tied down to a particular number of posts of responsibility, in the same way as a maintained school which had to comply with a particular 'formula' in the Burnham booklet. The salary structure could be varied to suit the staff available.

During the 1980s, a time of high unemployment generally, there was relatively little movement of teaching staff in either sector. Headteachers in independent schools had the impression that the less-taxing classroom circumstances of the teacher's job in an independent school were sufficient to retain the staff, without any additional financial reward compared with a teacher in the maintained sector. Children in independent-school classes were motivated both to be at the particular school and to learn, and this made the teacher's task easier. A great deal was expected of independent-school teachers out of school hours, but this was accepted as part of the job, and of the school's way of life. Mr Raikes of Waleyford Boys' claimed that teachers from the maintained sector applying for posts at his school did not have the chance to include in their *curricula vitae* the degree of commitment looked for at Waleyford, because the maintained sector had not offered them those opportunities. It was his view that while teachers in state schools were under considerable union pressure to withhold goodwill because this was one of the negotiating 'weapons' available, there were many in the state sector who were 'hungry for this kind of opportunity for commitment'. During a previous independent-school headship he had found that the energy of very good teachers was in search of an outlet, and these teachers were looking outside England or outside the maintained sector.

For assistant teachers at independent schools, promotion was no more easy to come by than in the maintained sector. Payment on or related to the Burnham scales ensured that relevant increments would accrue but gave no guarantee of promotion. Assistant teachers were not interviewed as part of the research, but there were some indications of a quiet undercurrent of dissatisfaction with the financial rewards of their tasks.[2] However, this was so overshadowed by the industrial action of the maintained-school teachers, in pursuit of the 1984 and 1985 pay claims, that employer/teacher relations in the independent sector appeared entirely equable by comparison. Head-teachers in the independent schools appeared to be trying to avoid a complacent tone, but were alert to the good impression which the undisrupted education and extra-curricular activities in their schools were making on some parents, when contrasted with what was happening in the maintained schools.

The question of a supply 'list' of teachers available to step in on a temporary basis was a separate issue. There was a clear difference between the two sectors in their access to this resource, and one in which the maintained sector had the apparent advantage. Only the maintained sector had an organised supply-teacher system. An education officer in Robart said that private schools in emergencies did contact the office to see if a supply teacher might be available. Such a school would not be put directly in touch with a supply teacher, but the office would tell any appropriate supply teacher that if they rang the independent school in question they might make a private arrangement with them to work on a temporary basis.

Several of the parents contacted in the research were qualified teachers, unable to work full-time because of family commitments, but prepared to do so on a temporary or part-time basis. It was normally in the maintained sector that they were called on to give their services, although their own children were attending independent schools, and it would have been equally convenient to work in that sector. One mother who in 1985 was just returning to supply teaching, now that her youngest child was three years old, considered it would be professionally unwise to accept temporary work in an independent school, even if she heard of an opening. Even if you did not 'declare' this experience, she contended, it might catch up with you and come out later, to bad effect, during an interview for a post in the maintained sector.

During 1984 and 1985, however, the 'supply' system ceased to provide headteachers in the maintained sector with the same access to back-up resources as they had previously enjoyed. Supply teaching was one of the marginal expenses of maintained education which was reduced, in preference to reducing mainline commitments, at a time of education 'cuts'. And industrial action by teachers, refusing to cover for absent colleagues, made it difficult to bring supply teachers into the schools without giving the appearance of 'blackleg' activity by the supply teachers concerned.

Method of selection and appointment of full-time teachers was another point of difference between the independent and the maintained schools. In the maintained sector, the Instrument of Government usually provided for governors to play some role in the appointment of assistant teachers, but this task was frequently delegated to the headteacher. However, he or she would normally be one of an interviewing panel which included local-authority advisers. During a period of falling rolls, the maintained school headteacher's freedom to choose staff might be narrowed by the requirement to redeploy teachers transferring from schools which were closing or contracting.

In the independent schools, on the other hand, the headteacher and the bursar were usually appointed by the board of governors, but all other teaching appointments were the responsibility of the headteacher. This put the head in a different managerial relationship to the teacher from that of a headteacher in a maintained school. As the headmistress of Broadacre put it, 'the buck stops here, at my desk. I have no cushion of the "Office" behind me. The governors leave the running of the school to me, and I am answerable to them'.

By contrast, the headteacher of a maintained secondary school explained that on the occasion of recent staff industrial action a letter was simply sent to parents informing them that the school was no longer responsible for their children at lunch time and parents must decide whether or not they could leave the premises. At the time this headteacher saw no need to become involved in 'aggro or anxiety' when teachers withdrew their services. This comment reflected the position which had traditionally been taken by heateachers in the maintained sector, that teachers following the instructions of their unions to take industrial action were in dispute with the local authority, not the school or the headteacher. However, the 1984 pay dispute was followed by the lengthy and hard-fought 1985 dispute, in which the government attempted to link the pay award with the restructuring and clarification of teachers' conditions of service. Industrial action by the teachers extended from refusal to supervise children during the lunch hour to refusal of cover for absent colleagues and a programme of short-period strikes during the school day. Headteachers in the maintained sector could no longer dissassociate themselves from what was going on. Both the National Association of Head Teachers (NAHT) and the Secondary Heads' Association (SHA) took a number of initiatives and became increasingly drawn into the teachers' dispute, which continued into 1986.[3]

Teachers working in the independent sector are to be found in the menbership lists of all the major unions[4] but appear to lack the solidarity essential for concerted industrial action. In an independent school any such action would be directed at the headteacher, and through him or her to the board of governors. This face-to-face working relationship may inhibit overt dispute. At the time of the research, the independent-school teachers appeared to be keeping their heads down about industrial action, leaving it to their colleagues in the maintained sector to make the running in the campaign for a substantial pay increase (from which all independent-school teachers on Burnham-related scales would also benefit).

Financial resources

We turn now to the part played by headteachers and bursars in acquiring and managing the financial resources of an independent school.

No form of education is cost free. Maintained education is funded from taxation at central-government and at local level. Until 1944 this indirect funding was supplemented by some direct payments from users, in the form of fees for secondary schooling. Since the 1944 Education Act it has been unlawful to make a charge to parents or pupils for the delivery of any aspect of the school's curriculum (whether teaching or pastoral).[5]

In the independent sector, the sources of finance are completely different. The lifeblood of almost every independent school is fees charged to parents. The fees for particular pupils may in some cases be partially or wholly paid by central government (assisted places or grants to pupils studying music or dance), or the local authority (places for pupils with special educational or boarding needs or in particular circumstances of hardship).[6] These payments are in the first place funded from central or local taxation but are in effect aid to parents rather than aid to independent schools. The general assertion can therefore be maintained that it is parents who control the supply of finance to independent schools. Some long-established independent schools have an income from endowments which is equal to or greater than the income from termly fees. Schools such as Hilliers and the Foundation School[7] are in this category. In the case of the Foundation School, endowments and 'presentations'[8] are used to keep fees low. There is a top limit of disposable income for parents eligible to seek a place for their son at the school, and all fees charged are means tested. In other cases of well-endowed schools, the fees charged to parents are comparable to those charged at other schools, and apart from some scholarships the income from endowments is used to supplement the scope and style of the schools' operations.

All long-established independent schools are not, however, richly endowed. The Waleyford Boys' School, established in the sixteenth century, had little or no income from endowments and was directly dependent upon fees from parents. The finances of the two Waleyford schools were managed by the governing body which they shared, and administered by the bursar in consultation with each headteacher.

The Waleyford Boys' School, like other HMC schools including the William Shakespeare School, was a charitable foundation. Other schools were also the subject of a charitable trust (including Culinara, Broadacre, the Zenith school and Mallory House), but not all had a bursar. Mr Standish, the headmaster of Mallory House, was his own bursar, and with the delegated authority of the governing body he dealt directly with the school's accountants and auditors. Cadogan, the co-educational pre-prep and preparatory school, had not sought charitable status and was run as a business by its headmaster, on his own behalf. The Philosopher's School was a charitable foundation and was run on normal fee-paying lines. Organisers of schools in this tradition were not entirely happy with the notion of prescribed fees and had experimented with a system of voluntary contributions. However, the acceptance of pupils proposed and funded by local education authorities had made the clarification of a prescribed fee unavoidable. Some independent schools (but none of those contacted in the research) were organised under a corporate deed of trust (e.g. the Girls Public Day School Trust; some minor aspects of financial administration were devolved to each member school, but fees including payments in respect of assisted places were handled by the trust).

The position of independent-school headteachers regarding the control of financial resources was similar to their control over the recruitment and management of teachers. In schools with no governing body, the headteacher combined the roles of owner and manager of the enterprise with the role of leading professional at the school. In schools where the head was the appointee of a governing body, he or she, with the bursar whom the governing body had usually also appointed,[9] had the responsibility of preparing an annual budget for the school which took into account current fees and feasible increases, desired developments in the school's provision, whether curricular, pastoral or recreational, and the allocation or use of any surpluses. Any difference of opinion or priority between bursar and headteacher would be ironed out before the budget was presented to the governors. Discussion by the governors would be chiefly concerned with alternative ways of funding the needs and commitments identified by the professionals rather than questioning the validity of their analysis.[10] This statement may appear to some heads of independent schools to understate the difficulty of 'getting money out of the governors'. But in comparison with the separation and impotence of most maintained-school headteachers in regard to financial decision-making, independent-school heads had far more direct control. Mr Ajax, the head of the William Shakespeare, who had spent much of his career in a maintained school, said that the speed and ease with which agreement to financial proposals could be obtained was in stark contrast to the maintained sector, where a proposal might await acceptance for several years.

The closeness and immediacy of financial decision-making made the management of resources a more satisfying task for the headteachers of independent compared with maintained schools. But several factors militated against a 'bottomless purse' approach to the raising of fees, the most obvious source of funding for new or increasing school expenditure. Since 1973 the schools, like other organisations, had felt the effects of inflation. Fees had had to rise steeply and for several consecutive years had moved forward at a faster pace than the rise in the cost of living. Schools were becoming aware of a limit of what the market would bear. Parents were not represented on the governing body and could not question the basis on which fees were established, but they might respond by giving notice to withdraw their child from the school. For the independent school, the survival tasks of ensuring a supply of resources and ensuring a supply of pupils were closely connected.

Another potential regulator of fee increases was the DES in schools offering assisted places. If, in the opinion of officials, the yearly increase in the school's fee was in excess of the expected rate, the school would be asked to justify this to the Department. Enquiries of this kind (with the implicit threat of DES refusal to match any subsequent increase with adjusted funding) did not take account of whether a school was, in its overall charges, 'cheaper' or 'dearer' than other schools participating in the scheme, but only whether the proportionate increase in their particular scale of fees was greater than the average.

In the 1980s there was in fact considerable variation in the fees charged by independent schools. Valid comparisons could not be made without a detailed knowledge of what was or was not included in the declared fee. Small differences could be accounted for by the inclusion or exclusion in the termly fee of school lunches or musical instrument tuition. Large differences could in some cases reasonably be attributed to the varying amenities and staffing of the particular schools. However, when all these things have been taken into account, independent schools could probably still be rated, like restaurants, into three groups as 'good value', 'moderate' or 'expensive'. Nevertheless, as we shall see in later chapters, the value of a school is to some extent in the eye of the beholder, the parent who evaluates what the school can do or is doing for their particular child.[11]

Apart from fees two other aspects of independent schools' financial budgeting mark them out from the maintained sector: their charitable status and their fund-raising techniques.

Charitable status

Charitable status has already been referred to as influencing the way in which schools with such status are governed and managed. The governors of a school with charitable status are appointed to comply with the terms of the school's individual deed of trust. But charitable status has other implications. Parents may perceive a school which has charitable status as being different in kind from an independent school run as a business.[12]

Bearing this in mind, the person responsible for the school's brochure may wish to stress the charitable foundation on which the school is based.[13] Charitable status also has financial benefits for the institution, and these have been repeatedly called into question by politicians of the Left. In 1985 the abolition of charitable status for independent schools was a tenet of policy acceptable to all wings of the Labour Party, and the Liberal Party and Social Democratic Party also had a policy of 'no subsidy'.[14]

Having charitable status is not in itself a way of acquiring new financial resources, but it does have the effect of reducing a school's outgoings on central and local taxation. The rating authority is required by law to reduce by 50 per cent the basic general rate charged to a school which is a charitable foundation. The bursar of the Waleyford schools pointed out that the charitable rate rebate applied only to buildings used for school purposes, not just for accommodation, as in the case, for example, of a master's house. One former benefit of charitable status has recently been phased out: exemption from the employer's surcharge for national insurance contributions.

Probably the most significant entitlement provided by charitable status was that the investment income of registered charities was free of tax. This was of great significance for well-endowed schools, but less so for those schools chiefly dependent on fees.

For Mr Standish of Mallory House, the prospect of losing charitable status was not one over which he would lose sleep. Financially, the significance of the status was only nominal for the school. The school could well afford to pay its modest local-government rates in full – this was one of the advantages of being on a small site. At other preparatory schools with more expensive grounds and premises, the loss of charitable status would mean a substantial rate burden. And at schools like Hilliers, he suggested, fees might have to rise appreciably.

Before the 1983 election, the Independent Schools' Joint Action Committees, which were set up on a district basis to campaign for preservation and protection of the schools, had responded to political objections to the schools' charitable status by emphasising what 'return' the schools made to their local communities. Independent-school headteachers, interviewed in 1984, responded to comments about charitable status by pointing out some of the reciprocal benefits which accrued to the locality by having their school in its midst. The headmaster of the Zenith School considered there was a growing pride in the school in the local area. Local-authority planners were kept fully informed about the school's intentions (e.g. plans to expand its boarding capacity) and were both sympathetic and helpful. The school tried to pull its weight in the local community by never turning down a request for a charity concert by the pupils. The headmaster of Waleyford Boys' stressed that the school was an important local employer and generated income locally through wages and salaries it paid and its own local expenditures. The benefits which Hilliers conferred on its locality were expressed mainly in terms of participation in civic occasions and in the giving of hospitality to representatives of local services (fire service, refuse collection, etc.) All the schools also made reference to community service by pupils to the local elderly and infirm and to other groups in need. These references were not, however, made as an indication of 'pay back' for charitable benefits received by the institution but stated as part of the schools' ethos (and similar community-orientated activities were referred to by maintained schools as part of their own pupil activity).

Fund-raising

A form of fund-raising which some independent schools undertook – the mounting of periodic appeals to parents, former pupils and friends of the schools, usually for the provision of a new building – was not a current practice in the maintained sector. In the 1960s and the early 1970s many maintained schools had raised funds for, and parents had often built, some extra physical amenity for the pupils, such as a small swimming pool. But since the onset of inflation and the decline in pupil numbers, fund-raising by parents and friends for maintained schools had gone towards the provision of mini-buses or durable goods rather than permanent physical amenities. Attitudes towards parental contributions to such amenities had changed in the increasingly harsh financial climate for maintained education.[15] Some teacher-governors took the view that it would be morally wrong for any money raised by parents or pupils at school to go towards some permanent improvement or addition to the school's premises which would then constitute an asset of the authority. This objection to enhancing a school for the benefit of future pupils was no doubt due to uncertainty in the maintained sector about the possibility of future school closures, when land or premises might be sold off by an authority. It was fundamentally different from the attitude taken by those contributing to improvement or additions to independent schools.

Parents valued the continuity of the independent schools as physical institutions, and the whole notion of appealing to former pupils for funds stressed this continuity of existence. In the maintained sector education officers and headteachers alike emphasised the changing fortunes and aims of particular schools, and considered parents to be misguided to base their choice of a school for the child on what that school had been like ten years before: 'Parents are always making choices based on out-of-date impressions. They have to realise that schools change'. Most of the independent schools, on the other hand, wanted to be seen as pursuing recognisable and distinct policies over time and laid stress on what the past had contributed to the school. These differing perspectives gave a separate character to voluntary fund-raising in independent and the maintained schools.

A further difference in resource management by schools in the two sectors was in the use they made, or were entitled to make, of support services provided by the local authority.

Independent schools' access to the services of the local education authority

In Morrowshire and Robart the extent to which local education authority advisers were an available resource for independent schools seemed to be a function of personal relations and the *raison d'être* of the school. The headmaster of Culinara found the local advisers responded 'very readily' to an invitation to come in. At the Zenith School two advisers from neighbouring and supportive authorities were on the governing body, but it was stressed that these appointments were in a personal capacity, based on these individuals' professional knowledge of and interest in the school's specialised teaching, and not on the advisers' positions in their local authorities.

A clearer policy position was held about the eligibility of the independent schools to draw on the authorities' school psychological services and careers services. The view was taken that the school psychological service was available to local children who were pupils in independent schools, but could not be called on directly by the headteachers of such schools. The approach must come through a parent. An educational psychologist would then, where appropriate, see the child and would advise the parent what educational changes, if any, appeared necessary. It would then be for the parent to negotiate these changes with the headteacher of the independent school, or alternatively transfer the child to a maintained school in the local authority of residence. The psychologist's advice would not be specific to the school in which the child was currently placed. In the maintained sector, if a child needed further help, this could be given at various levels. Morrowshire, for example, ran a peripatetic remedial reading scheme, but this did not extend to the independent schools. Any special help of this kind in the independent school would be a matter for negotiation between parent and headteacher. However, if the psychologist's investigations resulted in the identification of a statemented special educational need for which the local authority must take responsibility under the 1981 Education Act, it made no difference that the child had until then been educated in an independent school.

The careers service, like the school psychological service, was available for use by all young residents of a local education authority, even if they were not being educated in one of the authority's schools. Whether careers officers actually visited independent schools appeared to be a matter of custom and practice. The Independent School Careers Organisation (ISCO) is available to affiliated schools,[16] but several of the independent schools also had a long-standing working relationship with the careers service of the local authority. The school brochure for Culinara stated that county careers officers regularly visited the school, and the headteacher considered this the normal arrangement. At Waleyford Girls' School the headmistress was appreciative of the 'free help' offered by the local authority. One of the careers officers came regularly to the school to interview sixth-form girls and also attended parent's evenings. From the headteacher's point of view, this officer seemed like a 'part-time member of staff'.

Independent schools need the same kind of resources as maintained schools in order to survive – pupils, teachers and money. They obtain and manage these resources in characteristically different ways from schools in the maintained sector. Only in a few instances, such as the careers and other local-authority services briefly mentioned above, do they turn to an external bureaucracy to meet their needs. Most independent schools are, as we began by saying, fundamentally on their own in what they are doing. It is a situation which sharpens awareness of the *raison d'être* of any individual or institution. Local-authority schools tend to lack that awareness. If there *is* one system of education, its two sectors are more than superficially distinct. How do they seem to parents, who survey both independent and maintained schools, in search of the right education for their child?

SEVEN

Parental Choice: Themes of Transfer to the Independent Sector

Parents and their children's education

We turn now to a consideration of what the continuing existence of two sectors of education has meant for the consumers of education – parents and their children.

To obtain first-hand accounts of the impact of educational coexistence on families, it was necessary to move right outside the institutional framework of provided education, whether fee-paying or maintained, and make an approach to parents in their homes, where they could explain without inhibitions the factors which had influenced their children's education in independent, maintained or aided schools, and how the parents evaluated these educational experiences.

Education policy is one area where a good deal of lip-service is paid to those on the demand side of the supply-and-demand equation. Parents have been referred to as 'potential partners' with the school in the education of the child, and much interest has been focused on ways in which the educational attitudes and practice of the home influence the child's progress at school. A review of such enquiries in the 1970s indicated, however, that the concept of parents and teachers as partners remained more a theme of rhetoric than a reality of practice (Johnson 1982). In the 1940s the Fleming Committee had seen one of the advantages of bringing boys from maintained day schools into the public boarding schools as being the opportunity it would give such boys to make decisions about their lives which were not influenced by intimate daily contact with their parents. This implied view by the educationalist that the parent's attitudes may be counter-productive to the child's best educational interests has persisted through several decades, with the result that many enquiries into the relationship between home and school have been mounted in the spirit of 'finding out what the parents are doing and telling them to stop it'.[1] However, the competing notion that a child's education *should* be influenced by the wishes of the parents was enshrined in the 1944 Education Act. This idea, while rarely a reality in administrative practice in the maintained sector, has held its ground and has in recent years become part of a movement to strengthen parental rights in education. One theme of this parental-rights movement, to which we shall later return, has been the right of parents to play a part in the government of the maintained school. The other parental-rights theme, more central to the study of educational coexistence, is the question of parental choice of schools.

One of the reasons for the political survival of independent schools alongside the maintained sector has been successive governments' respect for the philosophical tenet that parents' choice of school for their child should not be arbitrarily restricted to the schools maintained by the state.[2] As we have seen, parents have been assisted or discouraged in various ways when considering whether to include independent schooling amongst their educational options. But the choice has always been there. In examining the experience of twenty-five families whose choices of schools for their children have extended across both sectors of education, our primary focus of interest is not the outcomes of those choices. The aim is, rather, to establish what factors influenced the sequence of choices for a particular child, and whether from the parents' point of view the coexistence of maintained and independent schools offered a wider range of choice or a larger number of offers by schools to do the same thing.

Twenty-five families

Through the local press, parents living in and around Morrowshire and Robart who had used both public and private education for their children were invited to send details of this. The selection of twenty-five families, from the eighty-five who responded, was based chiefly on the variety of patterns of use of the two sectors of education which these responses had revealed.

During the hours of interviewing which then took place in each home, parents gave much information about themselves and their circumstances, as well as about their children's education. To give some notion of the make-up of the group of forty-nine parents (twenty-four couples and one divorced wife) on whose experience this and ensuing chapters are based, some points are included here. Further particulars are given in the Appendix.

Thirty-six of the husbands and wives had spent their own childhood in the south of England, seventeen of these in the London area. Seven parents came from the Midlands or north of England, two from Scotland and two from Ireland. One husband and one wife (both of non–British origin but now married to people from the south of England) had spent their childhood in India and Egypt, respectively.

Nine of the families described themselves as having no religion. Eight spoke of themselves as Christian, and a further fifteen as Church of England or Anglican. Seven identified themselves as Roman Catholics and two as Methodists. Seven of the parents were Jewish, though not all practised their religion. One parent was a follower of a minority Eastern faith. In their politics, twenty-one parents were unequivocally Conservative and two unequivocally Labour. Six indicated their affiliation to the SDP/Liberal Alliance. Five would not acknowledge any political inclination. No less than fourteen of the forty-nine parents, during the winter of 1984 or the spring of 1985, appeared to be in a state of political indecision. They described themselves as Floating (six), Tory/Liberal (one), Tory/SDP (three), Fabian/SDP (one), Liberal/Floating (one), SDP/Floating (one) or Socialist/Floating (one).

Almost all of the forty-nine husbands and wives were in work at the time of interview. One couple had both recently retired, the husband having been a senior civil servant and the wife a part-time school teacher. In eight of the twenty-five families, the principal breadwinner was self-employed. (One of these was a clergyman; five had their own companies; two worked on a free-lance basis). In six of the twenty-five families, both husband and wife were in full-time employment. (In three of these families both were teachers. Two of the other wives in full-time employment were in para-medical professions, and one was a marketing director.) Of the remaining nineteen wives, one worked all but full-time on a number of part-time jobs, nine had regular part-time work, two had regular but minimal part-time work and three had very occasional work (all these three as supply teachers). One wife had occasional but substantial part-time work. Three wives were not economically active.

The husbands' occupation cannot be readily summarised. Several of the younger men (late thirties) appeared to be advancing rapidly in their careers and changing their jobs quite frequently. Two men who had retired early were now working part or full-time in occupations unrelated to (and less remunerative than) their previous jobs. Among the other husbands in full-time work, two of them were engaged on technical aspects of television and sound broadcasting, one was a minister of religion, one an inspector of taxes, one a senior nurse, three were in various branches of engineering (one as a consultant and two in management positions), one held a middle-management position in a large organisation, eight had senior-management positions or were self-employed directors in smaller organisations. Three of the husbands were teachers and one the principal of a specialist subject college.

Overall, the most prominent occupation in the twenty-five families was teaching. Eleven of the families had some substantial connection with the teaching profession in that one or both partners either was working or had for part of their career worked as a teacher. These included three families where both husband and wife were full-time teachers and another where both partners worked in a college of further and higher education.

The families' financial circumstances fell into three main groups. Eleven families had gross annual earnings of between £20,000 and £25,000. In all these cases, both parents were in work and their joint earnings were taken account of in the figures. All the teacher couples came into this group. Seven families had an income from earnings of less than £20,000 (mostly between £9,000 and £13,000 per annum) and in five of these the joint earnings of both partners made up the total given. Three of these 'lower earnings' families, however, had a further source of income from investments, which in two cases helped to meet school fees. The divorced wife, who had the lowest earnings of any of the principal breadwinners, had some help with school fees from her ex-husband. Six of the families had an income from earnings in excess of £25,000 per annum. In four of these the husband was a high earner in a commercial concern, and the move up to this income bracket was of recent date. One wife, herself not economically active, did not know what her husband's earnings were. He was self-employed.

From the variety of information about the families given above it is easier to sum up what they were *not*, as a group or as individuals, than to find common characteristics. They were not families of inherited wealth or following patterns of living established over generations. They were not unemployed or dependent on social security. Within these extremes they exhibited a quite wide variety of life-styles. On the whole, the younger ones looked on the way to becoming more affluent than the older ones.

Two characteristics of the group as a whole were unanticipated. One of these was the high proportion who were or had been teachers. Secondly, although all the families had by definition used *both* sectors of education for their children (and some had been selected because the patterns of use showed families had moved from the independent to the maintained sector, as well as in the reverse direction), independent education was favoured by these families in many more cases than had been anticipated. And some parents who had themselves trained and worked (or were still working) in the maintained sector of education as teachers nevertheless saw good reasons for using independent schools for at least part of their children's education.

The parents' own education had for the most part been in the maintained sector. Details of their schooling are given in the Appendix. The parents ranged in age from 35 to 62 and had of course had their own education at different times. From the accounts they gave, it was apparent that married couples did not in many cases share a common experience of a type of education. Some of the husbands and wives were fairly widely separated in age, and educational times had already changed by the time the younger member of the couple went to school. Their schooling clearly illustrated the very wide range of maintained schools which co-existed during the parents' youth.

Not only did the parents' own schooling experience extend over a number of years, and a number of educational policy changes, but the spread of their families in some cases meant that older parents were still involved with the education system at a time when the first children of parents twenty years younger were already starting school. Family size of the group as a whole was above average – between them, the twenty-five families had seventy-two children. These families had a lot of experience to contribute about the impact of changing educational policy on parental choice of school and many other educational decisions made in the family.

The interviews provide examples of nearly forty years of family decision-making about children's education. They cover the period when fee-paying schools of all kinds, including direct-grant schools, coexisted with maintained grammar schools, secondary-modern and a few secondary technical schools; the period of steep growth in school-age populations and the ensuing continuing decline; the removal of the direct grant to schools outside the maintained sector, and the gradual reorganisation of maintained and aided secondary education on comprehensive lines. At the same time, a number of organisational and philosophical changes were being made in primary schools.

Themes of transfer from public to private education

Families' reasons for transferring children to independent schools throw considerable light on how both sectors of education are seen from the 'users' point of view. Most of the families were influenced by more than one reason when they moved a child into the private sector of education, and we shall see later that the experience of one child sometimes had a domino effect for the education of other children in the family.

There were eight main themes of movement from public to private education. Four are discussed in this chapter, and four in the next. The families whose experience illustrates the eight themes can be broadly described as:

- Users and ex-users of direct grant or similar low-fee schools.
- Satisfied customers of the maintained grammar schools.
- 'Natural' users of the private sector (for whom the state system served as a temporary substitute).
- Aspiring users of the private sector (who considered it was 'bound to be better').
- Parents alienated by their contemporary experience of state *primary* education.
- Parents alienated by their contemporary experience of state *secondary* education.

- Families with boarding need.
- Parents looking for a school to benefit a problem child.

In the discussion which follows, pseudonyms are used to protect the identity of families.

Influence of the direct-grant system on parental choice of school

The direct-grant schools existed, under that name, for a period of fifty years from 1926 to 1975. Four of the forty-nine parents had themselves been a pupil at such a school. Three of the families sent one or more of their children to a direct-grant school in the late 1960s or early 1970s. For many more of the families an awareness of the existence of the direct-grant schools had given them a notion of an available private sector of education which was of high quality but moderate cost. This idea lingered on, giving a halo effect to what continued to be referred to as 'ex-direct-grant schools', and sometimes blurring parents' recognition of just how costly these schools now were since becoming fully independent.

Our review of political attitudes to coexistence, in Chapter 1, showed that tackling the question of the direct-grant schools was a political exercise several times attempted from the 1940s onwards, but not brought to the crunch until 1975. During the period that direct grants were paid to schools outside the maintained sector, some pupils from maintained primary schools were able to obtain completely free places at direct-grant schools as part of the 25 per cent free places the schools had to offer as a condition of their grant. Mr and Mrs Morgan benefited from this in the 1930s; so did Mr Joss in 1948 and Jennifer Verrall in 1963.[3] The direct-grant scheme also enabled local authorities to take up what were known as 'residual' places at the school. These were awarded on a means-tested basis. Mr Anthony had such a place at a direct-grant school in Scotland in the late 1940s, so did Noel Joss in 1977 (the final year in which the Robart education authority awarded such places). During Noel's time at the school the value of the award rapidly decreased as the Joss's joint income increased gradually, and the overall fee rose steeply. Mr Joss resented the fact that what his own father had got for nothing (i.e. a direct-grant schooling for his son) he himself was having to pay for, despite Noel's having gained an award.

Another effect of the direct-grant arrangement was to keep fees artificially low for *all* pupils attending the school.[4] Several families perceived the schools as 'reasonable' in cost. Mr and Mrs Roland had friends who had used a direct-grant school for their son. When Max Roland sat the entrance examinations of the Livery School and the Chapter School he subsequently attended, his parents were under the impression that these schools still had direct-grant status. When they found that the places which Max had obtained

were fully fee-paying and comparable with those charged at other independent schools, they were unwilling to draw back. Mrs Roland's promotion at
this time fortuitously enabled them to meet the fees.

Most of the parents who were aware of the relatively low cost of fee-paying
places in direct-grant schools got their children into the schools at the junior
department stage, partly to 'make sure' of a place at the secondary stage of
these popular schools and, usually, because they felt the child would benefit
from the preparatory education available in these junior departments. Colin,
Mark and Julian Barnett all started in the junior department of their school,
which their parents found was more expensive at the preparatory than at the
secondary stage, when the 'direct-grant effect' benefited all pupils. The
Barnetts had had their own education chiefly in the maintained sector. Mr
Barnett's work in the civil service required him to accept mobility as a
condition of employment. The Barnetts' use of the private sector for their
first three sons was, they said, because of the existence of the direct-grant
schools which they understood to operate a 'gentleman's agreement' to
transfer pupils between schools if a family had to move house, while the
availability of boarding places at most of these schools meant that a pupil
could probably be 'tided over' any vital period of his education. (In the
event, it never became necessary for the family to make such a boarding
arrangement, and the transfer arrangement did not work out.)

Some of the families began to use the 'reasonably priced' direct-grant
schools just before the junior departments' fees began to respond to inflation-
ary pressures in 1973–4, to be followed by the secondary-stage fees when the
direct-grant scheme came to an end. Peregrine Norland went to the Livery
School as a 9-year-old in 1973, and his sister Laura joined the equivalent girls'
school in 1974. From the time when she was notified of her acceptance at the
school at Easter 1974 to the time when she took up the place in September
1974, the termly fees doubled from £94 to £190. Some years later, by which
time Peregrine was 15, the parents were receiving an education bursary from
Mr Norland's employers. This perquisite of employment was not, however,
available when they first made the move to the private sector.[5]

When Darell Slieman went to the Livery School, getting a fee-paying place
there at age 11 in 1977, the fees were comparable to those of other independent schools, and they trebled during Darrell's seven years at the school. The
Slieman's would not have wanted to carry on with this expenditure as a
long-term commitment but felt they could live with it for a limited time,
particularly since the school was not, in their view, exhorbitant so far as
'extras' were concerned. They accepted that 'you always had to pay for
music', considered the meals reasonable in price and the uniform, only
required during the first five years, as not exceptionally expensive. Other
parents also referred to independent schools which had formerly been
direct-grant schools as being still moderate in their uniform requirements,
compared with other schools.

The direct-grant system represented what many perceived as the peak of what could be obtained via the maintained system of education. For parents with direct-grant experience, what chiefly lingered on was a feeling of excellence, of high-quality grammar-school education which could respectably be used even by those who were theoretically commited to the use and encouragement of state education. Parents will not choose between public and private education, with a consciousness of choosing between two totally separate forms of education, until the heyday of the direct-grant school has passed out of living memory.

Influence of the former grammar schools on parental choice of school

Nineteen of the forty-nine parents had been pupils at maintained or aided grammar schools, seven of them before or during the war and twelve in the years between 1944 and 1965, during which time all grammar-school places, like all other forms of maintained or aided education, were free to users.

About half of the seventy-two children reached secondary-school age before 1975, when there were still many maintained grammar schools in the area. Only eight of these children, however, went to grammar schools after passing the 11-plus exam. The remaining children whose secondary schooling took place during the 'pre-comprehensive' period either went to secondary-modern or secondary technical schools or were already in fee-paying schools by the time they reached the age of 11. Five of them moved to the private sector at the secondary stage because of boarding need or boarding desire. Several children had secondary places fully paid for by their local authority at direct-grant schools or Catholic independent schools. Two boys, however, moved across to a maintained grammar school later in their secondary years – Julian Barnett, whose parents were unable to arrange his transfer to another direct-grant school when they moved house, and Russell Cardew, whose independent school did not have a sixth form. His 'O'-level results were adequate to gain him a place in the sixth form of a local grammar school.

It is often assumed that families which have no tradition of using the private sector but where the children now attend fee-paying schools have made this decision because of the demise of the maintained and aided grammar schools.[6] Our analysis has shown that several of the children in the sample who reached secondary age in the relevant period either did not succeed in getting a grammar-school place or else did not seek to do so because their parents had already arranged for them to join a fee-paying school. These parents made little reference to the grammar schools. In two cases (the Barnetts and the Gracewells), where one son spent some time at a grammar school while all the other sons had different forms of education, the boys in question had not been happy at their grammar school. And in other cases, because the family had its sights set on direct-grant schools, or Catholic independent schools, or boarding schools, the question of whether a grammar-school place would be desirable was not debated.

Nevertheless, there were several parents who made a particular point of saying that their choice of a fee-paying school for their children was directly due to the termination of the grammar schools. Mr Winnicott stressed that 'if the grammar schools still existed, we wouldn't be sitting here having this [interview] conversation'. Mrs Peel deplored the end of a system which had served her older children well. The elimination of the grammar schools had, she felt, compelled her and her husband to spend money they could ill afford, in order to get their younger son a similar education to his older brother and sister in the only place they could now turn to – the private sector. Mrs Roland, too, stressed that had the grammar schools still existed it would not have crossed their mind to put Max in for entrance exams to what they thought were direct-grant schools (but which proved in the event to have become independent schools). Similarly, for Mrs Yalt the grammar school was 'where one went', and this is where she had anticipated that her children too would be able to go. Mr Yalt had attended a secondary-modern school, but he considered that the sorting out of children into different kinds of ability groups had been to everyone's advantage. Parliament had got rid of the grammar schools because they seemed unfair to those who took 'academic' and 'clever' to be synonymous and who found it divisive and derogatory to divide people up into clever and otherwise. But in Mr Yalt's view a child who was a dunce academically might be 'visually literate and as clever as the academic child but in a different way'. He therefore favoured selective education which sorted children into different groups in which they would be happy, but which did not take the line that one group was superior to the others. Children *were* in fact grouped within comprehensive schools, but this grouping was not an integral part of the system, as it had been with the former grammar, secondary-modern and technical schools. Those children who had formerly been able to move into technical secondary education at 13 no longer had this opportunity. It would still be preferable for selection of abilities of various kinds to be taking place.

Mr and Mrs Joss also regretted the end of the grammar schools. Although Noel Joss had gone to the school which his father had attended in its direct-grant days, there had been no long-term intention that this would happen. The entrance exam was only considered because his parents thought Noel temperamentally and academically unsuited to any school which was not academically selective, and this ruled out the comprehensive high schools which by now were the only form of free secondary education in Robart.

All these references to the loss of the grammar schools were made with heart-felt emphasis and were in some cases linked with another of the themes to which we shall later turn, that is, disenchantment with contemporary experience of state secondary education. But the lament for the passing of the grammar school did not by any means subsume all the reasons why parents had moved their children into private schools.

Personal attachment to the private sector as an influence on parental choice

There were among the twenty-five families some individuals who appeared to have approached their own children's education with the thought that private schooling would, either sooner or later, be the expected course of events. These parents were very few in number, and this is not surprising, since the criterion for eligibility to contribute to the research was that both private and maintained schools had been used. This criterion more or less ruled out couples who were ideologically or personally committed to one or other of the forms of education. But where only one partner strongly preferred the one sector or the other, their husband or wife had sometimes prevailed upon them to change their minds.

Mrs Gracewell was an enthusiast for the state sector of education, where she had had all her own schooling. Her husband considered that boarding school had been a good thing for him in his youth and was disposed to encourage their eldest son when he pressed his parents to let him go to boarding school. Mrs Gracewell was won round to the private sector by her first son's experience at the Foundation School and was happy to see two more sons go there. But for her the private sector began and ended with the Foundation School – a school with whose values the family were in sympathy, and whose means-tested fees they could just afford. There was never any question of the two sons who did *not* go to the Foundation School using anything other than maintained schools.

The parents who found it most natural to pay for their children's education were those whose parents had paid for them in their own school-days. Even so, their subsequent experience had led them to think it might not be necessary throughout the schooling years. Mr and Mrs Lennox had both gone to private schools. Mrs Lennox had then trained as a teacher and taught in maintained as well as private schools, latterly overseas. She and her husband had come to the conclusion that state primary education at least was 'probably alright now' and were prepared to give it a try. The nursery schooling which their son and daughter received in a nursery class attached to a local-authority school they rated as superb, but the subsequent primary school failed to stimulate Alexander. Both Alexander and Claudia were resettled in independent schools when each of them reached the age of 7. The parents had always intended to spend money on their children's education and had simply decided to do it sooner rather than later, in view of Alexander's lack of enthusiasm for the primary school.

Another parent who had had her own education in the private sector and had anticipated the same would apply to her children, was Mrs Anthony.

However, she did not feel strongly about this, and her husband took the view that maintained education would be perfectly satisfactory.[7] When Neville ran into a number of problems during his primary-school years the maternal grandmother urged that a boys' preparatory school be tried, and offered financial help with this experiment. From then on, Neville's education continued in the private sector. His sister Francesca gave no trouble in the maintained schools and had no wish to break away from established friendships. Many of her friends in due course left school at 16 whereas Francesca was planning to go on to sixth-form study. Her parents, and in particular her mother, felt 'guilty' that money had not been spent on Francesca's schooling in an equivalent way to Neville's, although she had, as her father remarked, received private tuition in music for a number of years. Given the opportunity to make a change of school if she wished, Francesca thought a couple of years in the sixth form of an independent boarding school would be a good idea – a proposal which was greeted with surprise and delight by her mother, who had herself had a boarding education. A case like the Anthonys demonstrates some of the complexities and layers of feeling which underlie most family decision-making, not least in the area of school choice.

The Ewells were another family which held different views about public versus private education. Mr Ewell's own direct-grant school had (unlike Mr Anthony's) made him a convinced adherent of private-sector schooling. In the event, because the children had to go to boarding school while their parents were working abroad, all their education was in independent schools. When this had to come to an end, on the family's return to the UK and the cessation of their employer's boarding allowance for the children, Mr Ewell felt dubious about the comprehensive school which his two younger sons then entered. Mrs Ewell, however, was glad that independent education, which was to some extent against her principles, was now ceasing for her children. She had a strong ideological attachment to the principles of maintained education and had found the attitudes expressed by other children in the preparatory school her eldest son first attended to be divisive and offensive. The secondary boarding school, however, although independent, had been selected by the parents because its pupil population was from all walks of life, many of them having their fees paid by local authorities, so this form of independent education had been more acceptable to Mrs Ewell. Nevertheless, it seemed to ease her conscience that her youngest son was to have all his secondary education as a day boy in a local comprehensive school.

The notion that fee-paying education was 'bound to be better'

This underlying motivation for a move to the private sector, sometimes expressed in the phrase 'you get what you pay for', was a clear influence in some families' decision to move a child or children from the maintained to the private sector. The individuals who voiced it had in most cases not been to private schools themselves. They expressed their opinions about the benefits of fee-paying education in a taken-for-granted way, making assumptions which the Conservative government's assisted-places scheme of the 1980s appeared to support, that 'everybody knows' private education is better than state education, but unfortunately only a few can afford it.

Mrs Cardew certainly wanted her son Russell to have a private education, and he went to the nursery class of a small private school at the age of 4. But her husband was 'against paying' and had insisted she put his name down for the local primary school. Before he was 5 'his name came up and they sent for him' to attend the primary school, somewhat to his mother's chagrin. Four years later she was able to get her husband's agreement to move Russell back to the private sector. Kathleen Cardew, a few years later, also went to the nursery class of a small private school and continued in the private sector of a fee-paying convent until the age of 16. 'Her father didn't make the same fuss about paying for Kathleen', Mrs Cardew recalled. Mrs Cardew was well aware that the private schools her children attended were not in the top flight. She would have preferred schools with more of a tradition of academic excellence. It was 'purely money' which held her back from trying to get her children into schools of this type, of which she perceived several local examples.

Mrs Cardew's educational decisions on behalf of her young children had been made from a background of an insecure childhood and a patchy intermittent elementary education which had frustrated her talents. In maturity she had reassessed her own educational potential, working through 'O' and 'A' levels to eventual graduation at the age of 55. Looking back to her children's early years she viewed her educational decisions at that time with some detachment. Her retrospective assessment of the benefits of involvement with private education, for a family with educational aspirations but no educational traditions, made an important contribution to the research.

Other parents who took it for granted that private schooling would benefit a child were Mr and Mrs Slieman, Mrs Uden (and her former husband), Mrs Ordwell and Mrs Dare. Mrs Dare's initial educational decisions were perhaps the most slenderly based. English was not her mother tongue and she had settled in the UK with her English husband shortly before the first child was ready for school. It was on her cleaning lady's advice that Mrs Dare sent Melanie, and subsequently Nathan and Desmond, to a small fee-paying pre-prep and preparatory school. Later on she was able to make more confident choices for her children concerning maintained and aided schools but appeared to have retained her view that private schooling was, *per se*, a better educational experience: 'Parents cannot tell what their future income will be. It seems best for children to have a good, sound primary education in the private sector, as with several children it might not be possible to keep them in the private sector all the way through.' The Dare family will crop up again in our later discussion of alienating experience in contemporary secondary education.

Mr and Mrs Uden, both of whom went to maintained grammar schools which they left at 16, had from the outset intended to educate their sons privately. This had been for several reasons: an unspecified notion of the 'benefits' of private schooling, the anticipation that the children would begin to learn foreign languages at an early age (important in the family business), and that in the absence of maintained grammar schools the boys were certainly not going to go to a comprehensive school. The private sector would get far more out of a child.

Both boys began their education in the fee-paying sector. Because of the break-up of the marriage, the parents' plans for their children were not, however, fully carried through. At short notice the husband declined to pay fees for either boy. Mrs Uden continued to keep Dennis at his IAPS school, but the older boy, Rodney, moved to a maintained middle school. By the time Rodney had had four years in the maintained sector, one of them in an all-ability secondary school, Mrs Uden felt fully confirmed in her early assumptions. She considered it 'a terrible shame for the country as a whole that state education should now be so far behind private education'. The two systems might well have the same aims, but children in the state sector (she concluded from her personal knowledge of the two boys' schools) were years behind those in the private sector. On the state side every child got exactly the same chance, but there were no opportunities for one child to develop anything in particular. Children were not all the same but in the state sector a child was never put forward a year. Mrs Uden also perceived a considerable difference in the disciplinary level of the two systems and the degree of involvement of the child in the school. When Rodney came home from school 'that was it'. Dennis, however, even when at home, felt part of his preparatory school. It was a continuous experience for him. But the overriding difference was in the level of education the children were attaining.

Mrs Uden's experience of the two educational sectors was contemporary with the research (and her assessment of her older son's all-ability school was, she said, further lowered by the teachers' industrial action taking place in 1984–5).[8] Mr and Mrs Slieman, however, had made their assessment of the relative merits of public and private education in the 1960s when their children started school. Mr Slieman's main wish for his children was that they should not 'be driven into industry', towards which he perceived some pressure by government and local-authority education. He wanted them to have a free and wider choice of career and concluded this would be more readily available in the private sector. Unlike Mrs Uden and Mrs Dare, the Sliemans considered that the greatest benefits of private education were to be had at the secondary stage, and must also be assessed in terms of the child's ability. You had to 'see how the children got on first of all' in the maintained schools, before moving them across to the private sector, which was more highly geared to competition. The brightest children would benefit most, but any child would improve with the support and encouragement provided in a private school.

Mrs Ordwell by contrast had taken the view that it was bound to be better for any child to start off in private education. 'The private schools seem to be able to get something out of the children which the state schools don't get. They live by different standards.' And parents, because they were giving up lots of other things to pay for their children to attend a particular school, would fight to get a lot more out of it: 'They expect a lot for their money.'[9] If there was 'the slightest case for their doing so', most children would probably also benefit from continuing in private education at the secondary stage. Nevertheless, the private sector did have 'an academic beeline', and a child with genuine barriers to academic work (like her dyslexic son Carl) was probably better out of the private system. With hindsight Mrs Ordwell concluded that a better route for him would have been state education all the way, supplemented by private tuition. At the later stages of education the value of private schooling had to be estimated not only in terms of what the school had to offer but also what the child by then had proved capable of. The appropriate outcome of a preparatory school was to move on to an independent secondary school of high standard. Other kinds of independent schools existed, ready to take 'the ones who couldn't make it', but there was, Mrs Ordwell considered, 'no point in this. They would do just as well in a state school.' Private education was not, for Mrs Ordwell, an end in itself, and she had no time for 'snob value'. Like most of the other parents who aspired to private education for their children without having experienced it for themselves,[10] Mrs Ordwell applied a competitive achievement model to her assessment of schools in either sector, although she noted in passing that her boys also learnt 'how to behave' from their school.

The case of Mrs Henry should be briefly mentioned in this discussion, although it will crop up again when discussing alienation from state primary education. Mrs Henry was a practising primary teacher in the maintained sector and did not approach her own children's education with the fundamental belief in the advantages of private education which was shared by the other parents discussed in this section. It was her children's early experiences which prompted the family to embark on private schooling. Mrs Henry, however, was quickly alerted to the existence of many families who wanted to use private schools but had little idea where to place their child or how to set about doing this. Mrs Henry capitalised on her experience and on her considerable professional and local knowledge of schools to set up a consultancy for parents and provide home tuition for children sitting entrance exams for private schools.

In several of the family histories so far discussed, as examples of families without experience of the private sector who aspired to use it for their children, there have been some shared features. These parents had in several cases come from homes where money was short or had had unsettled childhoods which cramped or blighted their own schooling experience. Two of the parents (Mrs Cardew and Mrs Ordwell) had been so permanently dissatisfied with their own limited early education that they had put in years of study as mature students. Mrs Henry, too, at the time of interview, was taking steps to add a degree to her existing teaching qualification and commented that part of her incentive to do 'the best' for her children was because she herself, in the absence of parental encouragement, had not done as well as she could have done at her own maintained school.

The final case to be discussed in this section, that of Mr Verrall[11] reproduced all these features and seemed a classic example of what is sometimes defined as the 'status-dissenting working class'. Mr Verrall, however, who had been politically active all his life as a 'working-class Conservative' continued to affirm his affiliation to and solidarity with the working class. His belief and investment in private education did not diminish his sense of identification with workers who preferred to spend their money in the public house. He felt he had the better bargain, but individual choice was paramount for him as a political tenet.

The study of coexistence in education clearly reveals the continuing influence of the past on the present. The educational policy to which one generation is exposed has an influence (not always an anticipated one) on the educational decisions which members of that generation make on behalf of their own children. The evacuation of children of school age, during the Second World War was one such policy decision which has had long-lasting effect. The educational history of the Verrall family aptly illustrates this.

Mr Verrall had been evacuated for three years from the age of 6, soon after he started school. Other parents in the sample had also been evacuated and had memories of the experience which made them determined that their own children should not have to go away from home to school unless they wished it. But for Mr Verrall the period of evacuation had completely changed his 'life, morality, achievements and ambition' by separating him from the values of his own family. Older brothers who were evacuated with him were gradually able to return to London. For three years he lived with an elderly couple whose attitudes to life, religion and the natural world were in total contrast to those which prevailed at his childhood home. Mr Verrall felt that in middle age he was 'still paying' for those three years away, in that from then on he felt like the 'black sheep' of his own family, different from the rest. His father he described as a 'coster-monger', a greengrocer with a horse and cart. Eighteen children were born to the family. Mr Verrall was the ninth child and several more had been added by the time he returned from his three years' evacuation. He passed the scholarship and got a place at a county grammar school, but there was never any question of his being able to take it up. The papers were torn up when they arrived, as he would have to leave school at 14. At 13 the trade scholarship (to technical school) was still in existence and he passed that too. For a while he worked happily at the technical school, then stayed away one day to help out when his father was ill. He never went back to the school and was soon expelled for being absent. He made his mind up at that stage that he would do better than his father by getting into the shop side of retailing. His subsequent rise as a self-made man with his own business cannot be chronicled here.

Mr Verrall stressed that throughout his working life his own limited education had gradually been compensated for by the self-education of being in politics. And he sought and took the advice of those he met, in the course of his voluntary work in local government, about how to give his own four children the best start in life. They recommended trying for a direct-grant school. The first child got a free place at such a school, through the local-authority system. Having once made contact with this type of education Mr Verrall decided to put his two sons in for entrance exams for similar schools at the earliest opportunity. They both entered the Livery School as fee-paying pupils at the age of 7. Fee-paying continued throughout their school lives, by dint of 'long working hours and no holidays' as the parents developed the family's small business. It was a matter of great regret to Mr Verrall that the youngest child, Josephine, was both unwilling and unable to pass an entrance exam into an independent school of good standard. The parents were not prepared to consider other types of private school where, as they perceived it, one would be buying 'snob value but not an education'. Josephine went to a comprehensive school which had formerly been a grammar school. Her experience is discussed elsewhere.

This section has illustrated that a number of different qualities were imputed to private education by parents who even though they had not experienced it themselves, nevertheless thought it had obvious advantages. For Mrs Dare, choosing a private education was the course of action advised by someone who knew more about the local schools than she did; for Mrs Uden it was a way of getting ahead; for the Sliemans it was a way of maximising a child's potential and opportunities at the secondary stage. Mrs Ordwell too anticipated that private education would make the most of a child, and thought that this beneficial effect should be latched on to from an early age. For Mrs Cardew as a young mother the private sector appeared to have had an instinctive attraction, and she may have perceived it as offering her children the secure and sheltered environment which her own childhood had lacked. For Mr Verrall, taking the advice of those with wider experience was the way in which he always tried to reach beyond what he perceived as his own limited frames of reference. When those whose opinions he valued recommended the direct-grant schools, he took their advice and was not disappointed.

In the next chapter we turn to the most unexpected theme underlying a move from the public to the private sector of education.

EIGHT

Parental Choice: Four More Themes of Transfer

Dissatisfaction with state primary schools

This important theme of transfer came from families who moved their children into pre-prep or preparatory schools not from any preconceived idea or personal knowledge that the private sector had a lot to offer, but because they had tried the state primary system and found it seriously wanting. This theme of exit from the state system at the primary stage was an unexpected one, for the popular impression is still in circulation, as it has been since the days of the Plowden Report, that maintained primary schools give great satisfaction, even if at the secondary stage parents have less confidence in the qualities of maintained education. Parents' references to unsatisfactory experience in the maintained (or aided) primary schools can be grouped under the headings of access problems, performance problems and managerial problems. These will be discussed in reverse order.

The 'managerial' dissatisfactions which parents had with maintained or aided primary education were chiefly situations where the head was promoting one policy and the teacher or teachers were pursuing a different policy. Parents were concerned about, but found themselves impotent to influence, what they perceived as a lack of consistency on the part of the school.

Kim Fellowes had a congenital physical defect which was being gradually rectified by successive surgical operations and the wearing of a body brace. Knowing that her small daughter had had a lot to bear in her early years, and that there was more to come, Mrs Fellowes wanted her to attend a primary school with a homely, caring atmosphere. The headmistress of the local infants' school explained her developmental educational philosophy and aims for the school to Mrs Fellowes, who found them admirable. The class teacher, Mrs X, to whom Kim was allocated, took a completely different line, using formal teaching methods and a sarcastic rhetoric to activate the class. The headteacher, when approached about this unanticipated classroom style, said there was nothing she could do about it. Mrs X had been with the school for a long time.

Mrs Lennox similarly found, at the first school which Alexander and Claudia attended, that the headteacher did not see himself as the leader of his staff. His initial contacts with incoming pupils and their parents were impressive. Each family was interviewed at length by the head, who was at pains to acquaint himself with the family's background and aspirations. After that, however, 'the curtain came down and you didn't see him'. As an ex-headteacher herself, Mrs Lennox perceived that this headmaster did not define as his concern the academic standards in the classroom. Management was confined to shutting the door and leaving the teacher with the children. What led to Alexander's removal was the complacency with which great variability in teaching style and capacity was acknowledged and ignored: 'Nobody at the school bothered, cared or minded. It didn't matter that the school, with a middle-class intake, was nevertheless failing to meet local middle-class aspirations.' Mrs Lennox served for several years on the school's governing body, but she and several of her fellows concluded that governors could do little to bring about change in maintained schools. The headteacher elected not to be a governor of his school,[1] but his presence nevertheless dominated the meeting in that the notion of 'professional judgment or professional discretion was drawn down like a veil' by the head if any change was suggested.

Mrs Lennox did not take the view that *all* maintained headteachers would treat each classroom as the autonomous sphere of the class teacher, but she saw that in the maintained sector a headteacher could get away with taking this line, whereas in the independent sector a school had to stand for something more consistent.

Another example of managerial difficulties in the primary school came from Mrs Tanner, who as a supply teacher more than as a parent had experience of several local primary schools. In one school, where she had worked before her children were born, staff had found themselves drawn into one of two factions – the supporters of the head or of the deputy head, who had opposing views of how the school should be run. Going back to the school seven years later, Mrs Tanner was depressed to find that the same disputes were still depleting the energies of staff and lowering the achievements of the school.

Mrs Tanner's teaching experience in the area had given her a clear idea of which schools she would or would not be happy to have her own children attend, and also alerted her to the fact that although a first and middle school might stand in close proximity and share a name, to be a pupil at both schools was not necessarily a smoothly sequential experience. Several other parents in the sample similarly found that first and middle schools, or infant and junior schools, differed greatly from each other in their educational approach.[2] Staff antipathies often existed between such schools, and these could affect pupils. Mrs Zaro found that the infant and junior schools which her child attended were completely separate educational experiences. Records and recommendations passed on about pupils transferring from the infants school were set aside and ignored by the junior-school head as a matter of principle.

Parents who had become alienated from maintained primary education tended to give most prominence to their dissatisfactions with the way the schools were being managed. In particular they were perturbed when those who should have been doing the management – the headteachers – did not see this as part of their task.

Another strongly felt cause of discontent was the standard of teaching and achievement in the primary schools. This 'performance problem' discontent was by no means entirely a backlash against progressive ideas. Several of the parents, especially those who had trained as teachers in the 1960s, were fully supportive of the progressive ideal in primary education.[3] Some parents, however, had found that progressive teaching, as interpreted by average teachers in average schools, left much to be desired. Mrs Keegan, before she moved to Morrowshire, had lived in an area where there were several teacher-training colleges. Through in-service training courses teachers in the late 1960s and early 1970s were being taught to teach in a new way, and losing a degree of confidence they formerly had: 'Everything that was previously sacrosanct in education was finished. Then, with the upset in the William Tyndale School, parents began to question what was going on.' Charlotte, the younger of the two Keegan daughters, went to a maintained primary school in 1975 and 1976; 'She wanted reading but they gave her plasticine', was how Mrs Keegan summed up her experience.

Another parent to whom the effect of changes in teaching methods had come home very strongly was Mrs Peel. Preston Peel attended the voluntary-aided primary school where his older brother and sister had been pupils ten years before. In Mrs Peel's view the school, in changing from its former traditional methods, had 'fallen between two stools, with the children not getting anything in place of the formal grounding they would previously have had'. In particular, insufficient scope was now given to bright children. The teachers, she thought, were right to spend time with those who were not doing so well, but should allow those who could advance ahead of the others at their own pace to do so. But this was not to be Preston's experience. He was 'held back' at the school from the age of 6. His teacher dubbed him 'the Professor' because of his vocabulary and grasp of English, but he was not allowed to progress to a new reading book because the oldest boy in the class had not yet reached it. The teacher explained this personally to Mrs Peel when she went to the school after Preston had been 'stuck on one book for weeks and weeks'. Eventually he was clandestinely allowed to take books from the school library provided he kept quiet about it, and the teacher stopped asking him to read in class so as not to reveal what he was reading – all part of the 'bargain'.

Reading skills, so often a cause of concern with parents of young children who acquire these skills only slowly, were a cause of rather different concern for several of these parents. Sensitive to the fact that teaching at home might differ from teaching at school, and thus might confuse a child, some of the families had deliberately held back from teaching their child to read before they started school, yet willy-nilly the child had somehow acquired the skill. Max Roland was such a child. His parents found the village first school could adapt to cope with children at different stages of advancement, but when Max went on to the more urban middle school, his by then well-developed reading skills were a positive disadvantage. If teaching resources were devoted to Max, to keep him working in the correct 'gear' for his ability, those resources were being taken away from other children who were lagging behind the average. This zero-sum situation in the maintained schools was referred to by several parents. Although theoretically equipped to cope with a wide range of ability, in practice the schools could only meet the needs of the children at one end of the range at the expense of children at the opposite extreme of ability. Mrs Henry was a practising teacher in the maintained primary sector. In her opinion maintained schools did not take account of the experience and stimulation which children in middle-class areas received at an early age, even if their parents were at pains not to formally teach them anything before they came to school. She found that the modern infants' schools 'started with the same expectation about children as might have been appropriate thirty years ago'. As a result she had seen toys being brought out, for the first class of infants, which the children had outgrown eighteen months before. The sparkle and enthusiasm with which children approached their school life could be lost within one term.

The views expressed by Mrs Henry, and by two other teacher-parents who contributed to the research (Mrs Tanner and Mrs Quex) were based on their current experience in 1984 and 1985. They worked part-time or on a supply basis in the maintained sector chiefly for domestic reasons, but were clear that they did not anticipate an eventual return to full-time work in the sector. Mrs Henry knew she would 'find the lack of academic standards too frustrating'. She preferred to spend part of her time developing the potential of those children who were brought to her for supplementary tuition, prior to entering the independent sector. In turning to the independent sector for her own children, Mrs Henry found that the qualifications, experience and interest of teachers at independent schools were made explicit to parents. This highlighted, for her, the 'secrecy' of the state sector's teaching operations where parents were distanced by the teachers' implicit attitude of 'leave us alone to do our job' and where, for example, the reading age of every child was an especially well-kept secret, *never* supposed to be revealed outside the classroom.

Mrs Quex, when she transferred her elder son Jeremy to a preparatory school at the age of 8, was, with her husband's full support, embarking on a pattern of education for her children which this family had never anticipated following. Not only was Mrs Quex an experienced teacher, she had also put in a number of years as an advisory teacher, helping other teachers respond to the challenges of progressive primary education. She now found herself in constant demand as a supply teacher over a wide area in a neighbouring authority. As Mr Quex pointed out, it was contrary to everything his wife's working life had stood for to remove Jeremy from a maintained primary school, but three years at school had taught him nothing. Informal methods did not suit him. He wanted to be taught things, not 'set the next page of the work book'. Jeremy was, Mrs Quex recognised, 'unfortunate with his teachers'. He was also unfortunate in that the headteachers of both the infant and the junior schools were nearing retirement and were not willing to take on the 'hassle' of enquiring into teacher methods or moving a child to a different class. Mrs Quex subsequently concluded that Jeremy gave a lot of trouble at school largely because of frustration. Eventually she took him to an educational psychologist for a day of tests, which he enjoyed immensely. Notifying his class teacher – who thought him backward – that Jeremy had a measured IQ of 140 did not help his relationship with the teacher, who subsequently threw a book at him and said, 'You're supposed to be bright, so you should understand what I'm teaching you.' Mrs Quex made an informal approach to a senior education officer with whom she was acquainted to see if a change to another of the authority's schools would help Jeremy. The officer commented that he was unfortunately unable to offer advice and help on a school change for a 'white and bright' child, though he could be helped if he were 'black, brown, deaf or below average'. Mrs Quex herself was paid by a local authority to teach, on a one-to-one basis, certain children who had fallen behind with their education. Forced to recognise that this level of attention was not available for the *bright* child in the state system, Mr and Mrs Quex embarked on private education for their two sons.

Mrs Henry had come to the blanket conclusion that 'the state system doesn't want the concept of "hard work" for children of primary age'. Mrs Zaro, another qualified teacher who had worked only in the maintained sector, found that it depended on the 'dynamism of the head' whether the kind of 'lively, curious, insatiable children' such as made up her family could have their needs met in the state sector. But Mrs Lennox, the mother of Alexander and Claudia, both now in independent schools, felt that there was another type of child who was abandoned to mediocrity in the state sector. The bright but lazy child, Mrs Lennox considered, really fell by the wayside in the maintained schools. The child who would not spontaneously do more than he was asked to do needed 'encouragement, exhortation, supervision, faith that it matters. I don't perceive the state system doing this.'

The third set of dissatisfactions which parents expressed about their children's education in maintained or aided primary schools can be described as access problems. Some of these dissatisfactions concerned the limitations on parents' access to individual teachers. Mrs Zaro was perturbed to find that open-evening appointments to speak to the class teacher at Damien's junior school were scheduled at three-minute intervals. She wrote to the school indicating that she had a number of points to raise, and asking for a six-minute interview. A formal reply was received to the effect that for any discussion longer than three minutes a separate appointment must be made for another occasion. For the most part, however, parents whose children had recently experienced maintained or aided primary education found that the schools did not unduly restrict parental contact with teachers. Whether or not such contacts enabled parents effectively to convey their point of view to the teacher, on any problematic issue, was a different question. The accept-ability of a parental voice, whether individual or collective, in either public or private education, is discussed in Chapter 9.

The kind of access to which parents chiefly referred in their discussion of primary education was access to a particular institution; in other words, the limitations which they experienced on the choice of primary school.[4] We have already examined some of the evidence which led parents to conclude that primary schools were not all the same. In many cases these parents, all of whom took an active interest in their children's education, had formed a clear opinion on which primary school they would like their child to attend. Frequently, however, and despite the provisions of the 1980 Education Act, they were unable to place the child in the primary school of their choice.

Teacher-parents in the sample were notably more successful in this than 'lay' parents, and this at both the primary and the secondary stages. Mrs Gracewell, a former teacher, looking back twenty-five years to the time when she was getting her sons into a variety of local maintained schools, concluded that in the 1980s nothing had changed. Those parents who 'knew the ropes' so far as the local education system was concerned, and were on social or professional terms with headteachers and education officers, had *always* been able to get their children into the schools of their choice. Other parents with less familiarity with the system consistently failed to do so. Mr and Mrs Joss, teacher-parents whose successful school choices had been made more recently, in the 1970s, took a similar view. Lay parents, they con-sidered, were likely to be less successful, but in any case they doubted whether lay parents were in a position to *make* an informed choice of school on the basis of a series of open evenings. All the schools looked good on these occasions, and it was only those with professional information who could judge what was really going on. Mrs Henry, a teacher-parent whose con-siderable knowledge of local schools has already been referred to, was also successful in getting her second son, Rex, into a different maintained primary school from the one his older brother had formerly attended. Having been offered a place at the school of her choice, she was even sufficiently confident to gamble on keeping Rex at his fee-paying nursery school for an extra term after the age of 5, thus making him eligible to go straight to the second year of the primary school in the hope of missing out some of the low-gear phase of primary education. Mrs Henry's gamble came off, and Rex duly entered the second year of the primary school. Nevertheless, it was her impression that the greater part of his first (autumn) term at the school was spent in making Christmas decorations.

One teacher-parent who was not, however, successful in getting a place for her eldest child in the primary school of her preference was Mrs Tanner. There were no official catchment areas in the local education authority by the time Ralph was ready to start school. Nevertheless, it had been the experience of Mrs Tanner's friends that, whatever preference their parents expressed, the primary places which children actually got were usually in the former catchment-area schools. Mrs Tanner did not want Ralph to attend the school in question, and wrote formally to the authority explaining why. The school introduced children to reading through the initial teaching alphabet (i.t.a.), and it was Mrs Tanner's professional opinion that the scheme did not work well for all children. She named two other schools in the authority which she would be happy for Ralph to join. However, the only place offered to Ralph was in the school she had been at pains to reject. Mrs Tanner considered that even by using the appeal procedure she would be unlikely to get a place at the school of her first choice, which was very popular with local families. She was not sufficiently enthusiastic about her second-choice school to set the appeal procedure in hand, so Ralph moved into the kindergarten of the fee-paying school where he had already been at nursery class. By the time Caroline Tanner was of compulsory school-age, Mrs Tanner had become aware that parents with church affiliations could apply to send their children to a Church of England voluntary-aided first school in the vicinity. Mr and Mrs Tanner were practising Anglicans, on the electoral roll of their church, and were successful in getting a place for Caroline at the voluntary-aided first school. Her younger brother, Alan, was likely to follow her there in due course.

This case exemplifies several of the factors which influence the exercise of parental choice of school. First, the experience of friends, alerting the parents to undeclared but effective limitations on parental choice imposed by a local authority. Second, the attempt by the parent to justify her positive choice (of two schools) on the negative grounds that they did not use the i.t.a. reading scheme of which she disapproved. (This may not have been the only reason for Mrs Tanner's rejection of the most local school. It evidently cut no ice with the local authority.) Third, the reluctance to make use of formal appeal procedures.[5] Most of the parents whose children had started or changed school in the 1980s were aware that choice of school, since the 1980 Education Act, was supposed to be a parental right.[6] However, scarcely any of them had used the official procedures,[7] preferring to try other more informal methods of achieving their goal. If these failed, a move to the private sector was often the next step.

Fourth, the case gives an example of a family taking advantage (in the case of the younger child, Caroline) of their 'special status' access, as practising church people, to a denominational school. This was one of several examples where families whose religion was an important part of their home lives had had no particular thought of using a denominational school for their child – usually because they considered that the home rather than the school was the place where the foundations of religion were most appropriately established. Nevertheless, when parental choice of school on other grounds was thwarted, they decided to use their genuine 'eligibility' (by virtue of church membership) for a place at a voluntary-aided school, such schools being perceived as 'a little bit different' in style from the general run. The voluntary-aided schools continue to stand apart, in parental eyes, from the rest of the 'state sector'. Forty years on from the 1944 Act, which attempted to rationalise the 'dual system' of maintained and church schools, the voluntary schools are still a separate thread in the pattern of educational coexistence.

Dissatisfaction with contemporary maintained secondary education

The themes of movement to the private sector so far discussed have already shown some overlap. Some parents who were 'natural' users of the private sector had also been dissatisfied with maintained primary education. Similarly, the theme of regret for the passing of the grammar schools overlaps with the theme of dissatisfaction with maintained secondary education in its present-day form. But these educational attitudes are not identical. In the case of dissatisfaction with maintained primary education, parents did not express a blanket disapproval of the stance taken by these schools (whether progressive or traditional) but rather objected to inconsistency due to managerial weakness, or low standards because of levelling down rather than fostering individual development. Similarly, with maintained secondary education, parents did not necessarily object to the idea of comprehensive education as such but rather to the kinds of institution which in fact emerged when the idea was put into operation.

Among the group of young people in the sample, there were several whose secondary schooling spanned the second half of the 1970s, when the re-organisation of secondary education was taking place in Robart, Morrowshire and many other local-education authorities. Parents of the young people who went right through these secondary-school years in the maintained sector of education did not have happy memories of the early days of comprehensive schools.

Reah Slieman, in 1974, was not given a place in any of the three comprehensive schools of her parents' choice. She went instead to a newly opened comprehensive, but her experience there was a disappointment to her parents. Subject teaching was not of a good standard, and the school lacked excellence. The children were of middle-stream ability, and in these parents' view could have done much better with teachers of better quality. No homework at all was set until third or fourth year, as a matter of policy. Some of the new equipment of the school was never unpacked during Reah's time there because the teacher either did not have the time, the skills or the inclination to use it. Reah stayed on at 16-plus to prepare for three 'A' levels but passed only one. In the parents' opinion the sixth form at this comprehensive was 'not a proper one'. Drop-out was high and not many went on to further education. All the groups were quite small, but there was no enthusiasm and little was done. However, Reah went on to a college of further education and got a higher national diploma.

Josephine Verrall's time at her comprehensive school was also unsatisfactory from her parents' point of view. They saw it as 'a failure from start to finish', especially when contrasted with their other children's experience in direct-grant and ex-direct-grant schools, to which Josephine had not gained entry. The comprehensive Josephine attended was chosen by her parents because it had until recently been a grammar school and had a good reputation. But the teaching staff were demoralised by the change to comprehensivisation, and many of the teachers subsequently left. Josephine had difficulty with all her school work, and in her parents' opinion would have been better off in a single-sex school as she was easily distracted by the presence of boys from the school work which she in any case disliked. She obtained two CSEs and one 'O' level and left the school at 16. Although she had been intended to do typing studies in the school's sixth form, she took an unskilled job and did not go back to school.

Craig Barnett had his secondary education at an all-ability school which in his elder brother Julian's day had been a grammar school. He considered it 'a dump', and when many of his friends left at 16 he did the same. However, finding himself unqualified for the kind of job he wanted, he soon returned to a college of further education, going on subsequently to study accountancy.

Deidre Yalt was also in maintained education at the time of secondary reorganisation. Her father had been a 14-year-old pupil when the school leaving age was raised to 15 and remembered the experience as one of being stranded in a school which was not ready to cope with the change. Mr Yalt did not want Deidre to have an extra year at the junior school, which had suddenly been relabelled a middle school, and then go on to a high school which had barely settled down to its new role of educating 12- to 16-year-olds rather than, as formerly, 11- to 18-year olds. So Deidre left the maintained sector for five years, returning to it at 16-plus when the sixth-form colleges too had overcome their initial uncertainties.

Turning to the young people who were still in secondary education at the time of the research, six of the eighteen children aged between 11 and 18 in 1985 were in comprehensive schools. Their education seemed to be proceeding reasonably satisfactorily, and none of the institutions concerned had occasioned the same impassioned feeling among parents as were caused by some of the maintained primary schools.[8] Mrs Uden was the only parent who currently had a child attending comprehensive school who was seriously dissatisfied with the experience. The unfavourable comparison she made between comprehensive and preparatory-school teaching has already been referred to. However, the remaining twelve of the eighteen young people of secondary-school age in 1985 were in fee-paying education. Ten of them had never entered maintained secondary education. Their parents' decisions that comprehensive schools would not meet these children's needs were based on the experience of other children in the family or of the children of friends, or the parents' own adverse experience as teachers in maintained secondary education.

Mr Winnicott and Mrs Joss were two teacher-parents who clearly expressed the view that maintained secondary education was unsatisfactory. Mr Winnicott had not wanted his son to experience the sort of comprehensive school he was teaching in. The able child was, he considered, positively discriminated against there. Slow learners were in a class of six, while ordinary, together with more able, pupils were in classes of thirty-six. The staff spent their time 'running around dealing with disciplinary matters'. There was no academic hurdle for entry into the school's sixth form; in fact, Mr Winnicott declared, his school 'would take a shaved chimpanzee with a blazer'. For their own sons the Winnicotts were looking for academic schooling. They wanted a secondary school which would consider a boy's strengths and weaknesses and develop whatever talents he had, a school where intellectual pursuits and academic-subject teaching were valued and where the focus was not on pastoral counselling and welfare. Such a school would be in complete contrast to the comprehensive school where he taught. Mr Winnicott did not presume that all maintained secondary schools were similar. Nevertheless, parental choice in the maintained sector was 'a tricky business'. In any case, the most visible local example of the kind of school he had in mind was the Chapter School, an independent (ex-direct-grant) boys' day school. The sons of friends were pupils there, and Sebastian when he reached secondary-school age was keen to join them. The Winnicott's impression of the Chapter School was that it had a strong academic tradition and, since it also had strong parental support, was able to leave the pastoral-care aspect to parents to deal with. The school was multi-racial, and there was a good relationship between pupils of all ages and teachers. At a school with this civilised environment of mutual appreciation between staff and pupils, boys could give expression to unusual ideas and find them accepted as interesting. Sebastian needed such an intellectually encouraging environment, the Winnicotts considered, to fulfil his academic potential. Oliver, on the other hand, was not so seriously scholastic, and did not spend his leisure on mind-expanding pursuits. If the parents could have got him into a maintained secondary school of their choice, he would, they thought, probably have flourished there. In the event, however, both boys sat and passed the entrance exam for the Chapter School. Their attendance at the school, though satisfying all their parents' aspirations for them, was placing a considerable financial burden on the family.

Mrs Joss was also a teacher at a comprehensive school. She stressed that her dissatisfaction with maintained secondary education was not based on comparisons with her own grammar-school education but on the decline in standards of the maintained sector which she had observed over twenty-five years of teaching. Teacher-parents had a view from the inside which was not available to non-teaching parents. She and those of her maintained-sector colleagues who cared about education sent their own children elsewhere. In her view many more people if they had the money would send their children to private schools. Mr Joss was also a secondary-school teacher in a denominational ('special agreement')[9] school. Parents using this kind of school appeared to perceive it as distinctively different from other public-sector schools, but in his view they were mistaken. The aims of non-selective public-sector schools could not be clear-cut, because of the wide range of problems with which they were faced. An additional difficulty for denominational schools was that the diocesan link was an impediment to effective educational decision-making.

As in the case of the Winnicotts, it was the elder son of the Joss family who by temperament and ability seemed most to need a selective secondary schooling. The Livery School at which Noel Joss gained a place was an ex-direct-grant school where his parents considered excellence in academic matters had been the stated aim for many years. The second son, Piers, also sat the entrance exam but did not pass. Neither boy had any special preparation for the exam, but in Noel's day the primary schools were still preparing children for the 11-plus hurdle, so he was slightly better equipped for the formal entrance-exam procedure. The parents used all their professional know-how to get Piers a place in the comprehensive school of their choice, and his education there proved satisfactory. He was an able boy with a more rugged temperament than his brother and would, his parents considered, have done well anywhere.

What can be concluded about the qualities of maintained secondary education, as perceived by these parents? All of them had used private education for one or more of their children, or for part of the schooling of the child who subsequently went to a comprehensive school and hence had some standards of comparison. They were not comparing like with like, but they wanted to be doing so. None of these parents took the view that private education was, *per se*, to be preferred, or had anticipated from the outset that they would pay fees for their children's schooling. In the accounts they gave of those young people who had by now left school, the personality and attitude towards education of the young person were more clearly perceived as part and parcel of their schooling than was the case in accounts given of younger children. And the eventual outcomes of the schooling of young people now in their early twenties, by way of further study or employment, gave the shading of hindsight to their parents' recollections of their time at maintained secondary schools. Also, it was clear that the time of changeover from ability-grouped forms of secondary schooling to all-ability institutions had been traumatic for teachers as well as pupils. There was a quieter tone about accounts of maintained secondary education which was still going on in the 1980s, and a recognition that some schools were working well. Even so, it was clear that some families and in particular the teacher-parents had experience of comprehensive schools where morale was poor, enthusiasm lacking and expectations low. Parents did not want these schools for their children. Lacking confidence in the feasibility of true parental choice within the maintained sector, some of them turned to the independent schools. Those parents who did succeed in placing their child at the maintained secondary school of their choice were generally satisfied with what ensued. We shall discuss later how the satisfaction of positive choice, whether for a particular maintained school or a particular independent school, appears to foster feelings of loyalty.

Moving to the independent sector to obtain boarding education

In practice, those families with a need or a wish to use boarding schools for their children looked to the private sector. They did not appear to have known of, or thought of using, maintained boarding schools. Nevertheless, a few parents who had no wish to use boarding education for their children remembered that in their own youth the threat 'I'll send you to boarding school!' had been sometimes used in working-class homes. Perhaps this use of the unfamiliar as a fantasy of punishment dates from the time when maintained boarding schools were first established. Mr Anthony, however, recalled that as a child the prospect of going as a boarder to a particular fee-paying boarding school with a spartan regime was sometimes held over his head, so some parents of a previous generation may have seen both public and private boarding schools as equally daunting. Going to a boarding school can be seen as an outcome of boarding need or of boarding desire. Although the two categories are not mutually exclusive, the two families who experienced a clear boarding need had no initial desire to send their children to boarding school, indeed they did so with some reluctance.

Mr and Mrs Ewell had embarked on a missionary career before any of their four children were born. Like all overseas workers in their missionary society in the 1960s they accepted the prospect of separation from their young children during school terms as an inevitable though regrettable circumstance of their work. Both these parents were Oxbridge graduates, and in the arrangements they made for their children's education they wanted to 'keep the road open for eventual university entrance if the young people wished it.' They also wanted to keep the children in touch with one another as far as possible and for them to be with teachers who had a positive Christian approach to their work. But the chief reason why the Ewell children went to independent rather than maintained boarding schools seems to have been the expectation of the missionary society.

The missionary society, although long established, had been dealing with arrangements for missionary children to have their secondary education in the UK only since the 1950s, when political events caused the society to close its own secondary school in the Far East, where missionaries' children had formerly been educated. The society undertook to arrange for teenage children of missionaries to attend boarding schools in the UK and to set up a holiday hostel there for the children's vacations. Missionary parents were nominally free to suggest boarding schools of their own choice, but the need to find a school which could liaise effectively with the holiday hostel gave weight to the society's guidelines to parents about the boarding education of their children in the UK, together with the particulars they gave of certain schools. For the society, at that time, boarding education and private education were synonymous.

The Ewell family's boarding needs were met, during the 1960s and 1970s, under the society's auspices. The parents were not, however, happy with the need for preparatory boarding in the UK, which seemed at first an essential precursor to Common Entrance and independent boarding school from age 13. They were the first missionary parents who, with the society's agreement, made use of an independent but co-educational boarding school which accepted boys and girls alike at age 11 and which had a more heterogeneous social intake than the schools formerly used by the society.[10] Other developments have since ensued which have further amended the society's policies about the secondary education of its missionaries' children. These include changes in the educational wishes and expectations of the parents, and the increasing reluctance of local authorities, in a time of financial constraint, to assume responsibility for the boarding need of expatriates.[11] For a period of nearly thirty years, however, the visibility, availability and Christian affiliation of independent boarding schools have been a benefit to the society and no doubt to other similar employing organisations. Changes in policy which may in the future diminish this connection are but one part of the uncertain future of independent boarding schools.

Another family who used boarding schools because of a period of work abroad, the Irwins, had less guidance from their employers. The parents had not realised, when Mr Irwin accepted secondment to overseas work on behalf of a government department, that secondary education would not be available for their children in the country concerned. The employing department undertook to pay the basic costs of boarding education while the parents were abroad. There was, however, no continuity principle of maintaining an allowance to the end of a particular phase of education, such as subsequently became the case for boarding allowances paid to servicemen. The funding would cease as soon as the family returned to the UK. In the event, Mr Irwin's one-year contract to work overseas was repeatedly renewed over a period of ten years, during which time the family's knowledge about boarding education increased considerably.

The government department gave no initial guidance or advice on the choice of boarding school. Their only criterion was that the school should be 'recognised' by the DES. The Irwins had no previous experience of the independent sector of education. Their eldest child, like his parents, had been educated at maintained schools. Nevertheless, in looking for a boarding school these parents turned at once to the independent sector. They found a place for their eldest daughter, Judith, at an independent boarding school for girls. The school's relations with parents were formalised, and the residential facilities spartan. In due course her sister Glenda, who had part of her primary education overseas, joined Judith at the boarding school.

During their time overseas the Irwins came in contact with many 'old colonials' who were working in the area and who had traditionally used the independent sector of education for their children. From these people and the children who came out to visit them, the Irwins became aware of the variety in the independent sector. When their third daughter, Penelope, was of an age to begin boarding while they were still overseas, they sent her to a different school from her sisters, a school where more emphasis was placed on the boarding amenities and care. However, a fifth child born in 1970 was by now approaching school age, and the parents decided not to accept a further overseas contract. On their return to the UK the support for the two girls still in boarding school immediately ceased. The local education authority in which the family had their UK home was eventually prevailed upon to pay part of Glenda's fees while she completed her 'O' level course, but she left the boarding school and transferred to the maintained sector at 16, and Penelope left her even more expensive boarding school after only one year to attend a maintained high school.

The family had no complaints about those parts of their daughters' education which were provided in the maintained sector, and they considered the maintained provision to be greatly improved since their eldest son's time in the system (1954–65 approx.), but their memories of the variety of schools attended by the children of families' with longer-term residence overseas remained, as well as the impression of a greater flexibility and ability to meet individual need in the independent sector. When Adrian, so much younger than the rest of the family that he seemed like an only child, appeared apathetic in his maintained primary school, Mrs Irwin revived her memories of some self-possessed children who had come on holiday overseas from their progressive boarding school, Culinara, and went to see the school on Adrian's behalf. The school was costly and there was now no funding from an employer. But in the parents' opinion the school provided Adrian with the self-motivating environment he needed, encouraging his maturity as an individual, away from family ties. Boarding was the right decision for him, and the school was well worth paying for.

For the Irwins the opportunity to use independent boarding schools at reduced cost[12] served as an introduction to a type of education which they would not have considered under other circumstances. It made them aware of the individuality of certain independent schools, the *raisons d'être* discussed in Chapter 4, with the result that they were later prepared to meet the full cost of one child's independent boarding education – the only family in the sample to do so.

The Gracewells had no boarding need. They lived in an area to which they had returned at least partly because of their knowledge of the good maintained schools in the locality. Yet three sons of the family went away from home to the Foundation School, a famous boarding school for boys. It could be said that boarding came as part of the 'package', but in fact the family's first approach to the school had been specifically because the eldest son wanted to attend a boarding school. He got the taste for boarding during a brief one-term stay at a boarding preparatory school whilst his parents were moving house, but perhaps a stronger influence was that his father had himself attended a boarding school in Ireland and had mainly happy memories of his experience. Mrs Gracewell, a former teacher in the state sector, was initially somewhat opposed to any form of private education, let alone boarding. However, the Foundation School became a valued part of the family's life, with three sons going there in turn.

There was no indication that the Gracewells gave any thought to the possible availability of a boarding place at a maintained school, when Rufus first expressed his wish for a boarding school education in the mid-1960s. Equally, however, the family did not respond by surveying the whole field of private-sector boarding. They were of limited means, and most boarding schools were financially out of the question. If Rufus was to have his wish, he had to gain a place which would be means-tested, where his financially limited family circumstances did not stand out from those of the other boys and, most important to his parents, where the religious values and Christian atmosphere of the school would match those of the home. Only the Foundation School fulfilled all these criteria. Its Christian ethic was a prominent feature, and its competitive entry was restricted to boys of ability from low-income families.

Since the Gracewell's case evinced no boarding need, only boarding desire, they would not have been eligible for local-authority help with boarding fees, even at a maintained boarding school, and it seems unlikely that the maintained schools of this kind which did exist in their area would have fully matched all their criteria in the way that the Foundation School did.

From the cases quoted there is some evidence that the distinctive *raisons d'être* of particular independent boarding schools justified in parent's minds the inevitably high costs of boarding, whether borne by school, local authority or family, or a combination of all three. Maintained boarding schools do not appear to lay similar stress on distinctive institutional style.[13] In the absence of a clear *raison d'être* which commends itself to education committee members as well as parents, it is perhaps not surprising that fewer and fewer local authorities seem prepared to persevere with the high cost of running a maintained boarding school. Although the costs are partly mitigated by inter-authority recoupment and parental contributions, the concomitant administrative problems are considerable.[14]

Looking for a school to benefit a problem child

This final theme, as a rationale of movement from the public to the private sector of education, cropped up in several accounts. As a reason for changing schools it is probably one which least endears parents to teachers or education officers. 'What makes them think their child is so special?' Lengthy interviews, however, put the parents' assessment of a particular child's qualities in the context of all their parental experience. They demonstrated that there are many interactive reasons why one family experiences as a problem a situation which another family might take in its stride. These examples of family psychology cannot be fully explored here. Our interest is in the role which the private sector of education played in solving or ameliorating these family problems.

The cases which most obviously presented their families with a problem were two children with special educational needs: Deborah Keegan, handicapped by the Downs syndrome, and deeply autistic Stephen Morgan. Neither of them, however, aptly illustrates the theme we are exploring here of families who turned explicitly to the private sector for help with their problems. Just as, when cases of special educational need were discussed in local authorities' educational sub-committees, the question of whether a handicapped child's needs were to be met in private- or public-sector schools was fairly uncontroversial, so in these two cases the fundamental obviousness of the child's needs held centre stage. The question of whether those needs were to be met in the maintained or non-maintained schools was peripheral to the parents' concern.

This would not always have been so. Deborah Keegan and Stephen Morgan were both 19 in 1985. Their births in 1966 came at a time when the responsibilities assumed by central and local government for the education of handicapped children were in the throes of rapid change. Developments have continued through the ensuing years, urged on by the pressure-group and charitable activities of families like the Keegans and the Morgans.[15] Deborah Keegan had all her special education in local-authority schools. Stephen's day care was the responsibility of the local health authority until he reached the age of 7.[16] From 1973 onwards the local education authority paid for him to attend a newly opened non-maintained education centre for autistic children, fees at which were, as Mrs Morgan commented, 'more expensive than Eton'. The costs to the parents of bringing these young people to the educational stage they had reached in 1985 had not been financial.[17]

The kind of problems which had caused parents (including the Keegans for their other daughter Charlotte) to look in the direction of private schools had been behavioural problems, which in several cases were perceived by the parents as allied with 'giftedness'. A principal educational psychologist who contributed to the research was firmly of the opinion that 'high intelligence is not a problem'. This view would not have been shared by all the parents interviewed. The intellectual capacity of Charlotte Keegan, Jeremy Quex and Damien Zaro was perceived by their parents as the underlying cause of their frustrations at school and sometimes at home. In each case the wide-ranging intellectual appetites, and the physical energies of these children seemed eventually to find satisfaction in independent schools which worked a long day, had numerous extra-curricular activities and encouraged physical recreation of all forms. The children were still perceived as exhausting members of the family, but the unhappiness they had experienced and created when in their previous undemanding schools appeared to have been dissipated.

Not all the children who gave problems while being educated in the maintained sector were perceived as unusually bright. In a family which values education highly, a child who does not like school is by definition a cause of some concern. Alexander Lennox's parents did not think that the move from a maintained primary to an independent preparatory school would necessarily change their son's passive but growing resistance to the pupil role, but they were delighted when it did. Nelson Anthony was another boy who seemed to be determined not to take his schooling seriously. Having grown extremely rapidly, his height made him a figure of fun for his school fellows. He responded by adopting with enthusiasm the behaviour of the class clown, and by the age of 10 he seemed set to pass through his maintained secondary education stereotyped into that role. A move to an independent preparatory school gave him a fresh start, and the opportunity to excel in sport and reach the peak of what his parents perceived as his moderate intellectual achievement. What made the difference, in their view, was that the independent school 'did not give up on people'.

Desmond Dare appeared to have been a problem child from birth – 'the pain of my life', said his mother. His timidity and emotional instability during childhood meant that his early years at a private pre-prep and preparatory school were far from uneventful. At the age of 11 he followed his brother Nathan to a voluntary-aided secondary school which had recently become fully comprehensive. His development into an obsessively neat and clean adolescent was not well tolerated by his school-fellows, and much bullying ensured, to which his teachers' response was that 'Desmond must learn to be like the others.' Mrs Dare thought this outcome unlikely and possibly undesirable. She approached another comprehensive school with a view to transferring him. The school was sympathetic to Desmond's problem but unable to offer him a place that term. Desmond transferred instead to a small unpretentious private school for boys where with encouragement and a quiet life he began gaining confidence. When the comprehensive school came up with the offer of a place the following term, his parents decided to leave him in the private school.

In no case did the move to the private sector mean that the education of these erstwhile problem children became entirely smooth running. But once the parents had found schools which acknowledged the individuality of their child, they seemed more tolerant of weak points in the schools' provision than they had previously been in the maintained sector. Loyalty was beginning to be established.

NINE

Parental Choice: The Threshold of Affordability

Financial considerations

Any discussion of parental choice between the public and private sectors of education has to take account of financial considerations. Fee-paying is one of the principal arguments against the continuation of educational coexistence. It is held to be unfair for people who can afford private education to be able to choose between the sectors, while for those who cannot afford it choice is restricted to the maintained or aided schools. Another relevant argument, and one used by those who wish to see the continuation of educational coexistence, is that public money can and should be used to make private education accessible to at least some families who wish to use it but cannot afford it. The latter argument was, in the past, the basis for the funding of direct-grant schools and the various assisted-places schemes which some local authorities used to operate. In the 1980s the continued existence of DES grants for places at specialised private institutions for students with a talent for music or dance, the government's assisted-places scheme and the payment by local authorities for places for children with boarding need, all work towards making private education a possible alternative for some people who want it but cannot afford it.

In discussing financial considerations with parents two points were of particular salience. First, what were the sources of finance on which they drew in paying school fees, and second, was there a 'threshold of affordability' below which the use of private education was considered out of the question?

Fees charged to parents interviewed who had children in the independent

117

sector in 1985 were of the order of £5,000 per annum (with extras) for a secondary boarding place, £2,000 to £2,500 at a boys' secondary day school, and from £1,500 at a preparatory school.

None of the parents were persons of inherited wealth, in the sense of having invested capital which they anticipated passing on intact to their heirs, having used only the income from it. One or two of the parents nearing middle age had received legacies from their own parents. In most cases these had come after any children for whom fees were paid had completed the greater part of their education. In other cases it was anticipated that both the income from and the capital sum of the legacy would be drawn on to meet continuing school fees. For the most part, all the families were meeting or had met fees chiefly from earned income (usually the income of both partners) or earned income subsequently invested, with small contributions from other sources. Figure 2 summarises the sources from which some families had help with school fees.

None of the families had applied for an assisted place under the scheme laid down by the 1980 Act. All the local-authority-funded places in Column (a) of Figure 2 have been discussed in earlier chapters. They were either places taken up by local education authorities at independent or direct-grant schools before this practice was discontinued in the mid-1970s, or places paid for by local authorities because of boarding need or special educational need. Merit scholarships, shown in column (b), were in most cases small exhibition

Parent No.*	(a) LEA funded places	(b) Merit schol. awarded by school	(c) Reduced fees for additional children at same school	(d) Reduced fees related to parental means	(e) Grant from a Charity	(f) Grant from Employer	(g) Financial help from family.
★ See Appendix, Table B.			FOR CHILDREN WHO LEFT SCHOOL BEFORE 1985				
2				✔			✔ (friend)
3		✔	✔				
6							✔
11	✔	✔		✔			
12	✔	✔					
13	✔					✔	
17	✔					✔	
19		✔				✔	
24	✔						
			FOR CHILDREN STILL AT SCHOOL IN 1985				
5						✔	
6		✔					✔
11	✔						
17						✔	
21			✔				
25				✔	✔		

Figure 2 Parents who had some financial help with school fees.

awards which made nominal acknowledgement of the abilities or achievements of the young people concerned. The only pupil to have full fees remitted by the school on a basis of merit was Colin Barnett, who in 1962 at the age of 13 was given a full scholarship by the direct-grant school whose junior and senior departments he had been attending since the age of 7. By the 1980s it seemed that full scholarships to independent schools, based on merit and unrelated to parental means, were a thing of the past. Partial bursaries or scholarships were still available to be competed for, however; but the only way an able child could obtain full remission of fees at an independent school was if they obtained a place at one of the schools participating in the government's assisted-places scheme, and parental income was so low as to rule out all parental contribution. The headmaster of Waleyford Boys' School commented that although his school, for example, offered a number of scholarships and bursaries, it was not the school's policy to recruit clever boys by offering places which were totally free of cost to parents.

The reduction in fees to families who had more than one child at the same independent school, shown in Column (c), were in both cases nominal (about £50 per annum off the fees of the second child in 1984). None of the scholarships or fee reductions in Columns (b) or (c) were perceived by families as having had any major effect on the intention to use or continue using the independent school in question.

The means-related fee reductions, shown in Column (d), were more important in their influence on the school careers of some children. The Gracewell boys, for example, would never have gone to the Foundation School had the fees not been means-related. The temporary reduction in fees accorded to Mrs Uden by her son's preparatory school at a time of family difficulties made it possible for Dennis to remain at the school (with the additional short-term help of a charity) while negotiations took place between his estranged parents. And places for two of the Morgan sons might not have been sought at the independent school where their father was a teacher, had it not been for the fee reduction from which he benefited.[1]

The remaining important potential sources of financial help with school fees to which no reference has yet been made in any of the accounts of children's independent schooling were family help and grants from employers, as a perquisite of a parent's seniority of employment.

Almost all the families affirmed with feeling that they had neither asked for nor received any financial help with school fees from family members. Most of the parents were first-time users of the fee-paying sector, with no precedent in the family for inter-familiar assistance of this kind. Having made the decision to use private schools, the parents felt it was up to themselves to meet the costs involved. In one or two cases, however, older relatives made spontaneous offers of financial help. One grandfather made a small covenant in favour of his grandson who had transferred to a fee-paying preparatory school. And in the Anthony family, relatives, including the grandparent who had urged his parents to consider an independent school for Neville, sub-sequently made regular contributions to the fees paid for him and later for his sister.

The two families where the father became eligible for employer assistance with school fees had already embarked on the use of private-sector schools for their children. One of the employers concerned gave employees at or above a particular managerial level the opportunity to apply for a grant of respect-ively one-third of the school fees for children over the age of 7, and a 'fixed sum' bursary (in accordance with tax-law requirements) which in the case of the family concerned covered 50 per cent of their expenditure for the preparatory school attended by their fourth child in 1985. This family had benefited from bursaries since 1978, at which time their eldest children had already been at fee-paying schools for five or six years. Initially, the bursaries covered full fees and were adjusted in line with fee increases. Latterly, however, taxation requirements had greatly reduced the scope of the bursaries.[2]

This account shows that the most readily envisaged forms of private help to parents paying school fees – financial help from family or employer – were not of major significance in influencing any of these twenty-five families' use of private sector schools, and in most cases did not play any part at all. The only substantial sources of help had been the local education authority grants in respect of direct grant and other selected independent schools, grants which were discontinued following the 1975 Education Act. Those families who were paying for their children to attend independent schools in the 1980s were setting aside a substantial proportion from relatively modest earnings in order to do so.

The 'threshold of affordability' at which a family felt it feasible at least to investigate the possibilities of fee-paying education could not be established at a particular figure. Families making the first move to the private sector appeared to have taken into account the age of older children and the stage they had reached in life, in particular the degree of parental support they were likely to continue to need. The Peel family, for example, said that Preston's application to an independent secondary school could only be contemplated because his brother and sister were by then in their early twenties and, although until recently in higher education, were not now a major charge on the family budget. The question of how long the fee-paying period was likely to last was also a consideration for families, although some parents seemed to prefer not to calculate for how many years their means would be straitened by this outlay.

Only one of the families had made any long-term advance arrangements to have money available for school fees. Although such tax-efficient schemes are widely advertised, it was not surprising that they had not been embarked on, since for most of these families there had been no expectation that private education would be used, indeed there was rather a clear intention that children of the family would be educated in state schools. Shortly after the interviews with parents were completed, a new loan scheme was launched for families who had made no advance preparation for the payment of school fees and who wanted to spread the load of fee-payment over an extended period. The scheme met with a popular response. It seems likely therefore that the parents discussed in this book were not untypical of many others in having made unanticipated and unplanned-for use of private schools for their children's education.

Several families said that the threshold of affordability for contemplating private education was reached by the adjustment of certain priorities. Home refurbishment, running a car and family holidays were all referred to as having been set aside in order to meet school fees. Family savings and part-time or full-time earnings of the mother as well as the father's income from employment were all drawn on by fee-paying parents. Several parents explicitly stated that rather than withdraw their children from fee-paying schools, they would realise capital by selling their homes and moving somewhere smaller.

Some of the decisions to move children from maintained to independent schools had been made at moments of crisis and put into effect with celerity. Parents then sometimes found they had embarked on something bigger than they had bargained for, in that they felt compelled to undertake a similar outlay for other children in the family whose maintained education had not so far occasioned any particular difficulty. The 'domino effect' of one child's education on another's was not, however, confined to the crisis cases.

The domino effect

Parental choices in education are sometimes made only for the first child in the family. Johnson and Ransom (1983) found that brothers and sisters frequently followed one another to the maintained school which was originally selected with the individual needs of the first child in mind. Patterns of use of the public and private sector of education and of particular independent schools proved to be subject to the same domino effect. Jennifer Verrall's secondary education at a direct-grant school led the way for her two brothers' education in the independent sector from the age of 9; Laura Norland went to the Livery School for Girls a year after her brother went to the equivalent boys' school, and Denzil Norland was subsequently started in the fee-paying sector from the age of 4. Carl Ordwell was transferred from a maintained primary to a fee-paying preparatory school. His brothers, Donald and Murray, joined the same school at the pre-prep stage. Russell Cardew was switched to the private sector at age 9; Kathleen Cardew was privately educated from the outset. Alexander Lennox moved to a fee-paying school when 7 years old. His sister Claudia made a similar transfer at the same age, two years after Alexander.

These were all cases where the outcomes of a first-time use of the private sector for the new generation had convinced parents that independent schools were worth paying for and should, where possible, be used for other children. A different kind of domino effect was experienced when a younger child of a family expressed a positive wish to attend the same fee-paying school as an older sibling and the parents felt impelled to let him[3] follow suit, thus almost doubling their original envisaged expenditure on fees. In one case the parents allowed the younger son to take the entrance exam for the independent selective school attended by his able older brother, with no expectation that he would succeed. When he gained a place the health and earning power of both partners became crucial in keeping the family solvent during the five years when both boys were at the school.

In other cases, parents paid fees for a second child because it was 'only fair' to spread expenditure evenly over both (or all) members of the family.[4] But if entry was highly academically selective, parents whose subsequent children were allowed to attempt entrance to a school attended by an older sibling but failed to gain a place appeared in several cases to feel absolved from the pressure to spend equal money on all children.

The financial considerations which influenced families' use of private schools for their children have been shown to be both interactive and complex. From the point of view of those charging fees for education it is, however, of interest to note that a family's first-time expenditure of this kind is usually not its last. Parents do not necessarily wait to see the outcome of the education of the first child for whom fees are paid before offering the same opportunity to other children in the family.

The role of the maintained sector of education for families who had passed the threshold of affordability

With the exception of three who transferred at 16-plus for particular courses, the maintained education received by those children who had previously had at least part of their education in private schools was perceived by their parents as a second-best experience. And no child who had his or her secondary education, or indeed *all* his or her education, in the maintained sector was seen as having been better off than brothers and sisters in the private sector or even as having had a comparable experience. Although these families had not all started out with the assumption that private education was better than public education, in their actual experience they found it so.

The coexistence of maintained with private education did, however, have many practical advantages for these families. It meant, for example, that they did not have to pay for *all* their children's education, nor pay for all of any one child's education throughout the compulsory schooling years, if they did not wish to do so. The maintained and aided schools were always there. In some cases these schools served as a springboard from which a child might seek entry to an academically selective independent school. Sebastian and Oliver Winnicott did this. Their parents stressed that these boys had no special tutoring or preparation for the Chapter School's entrance exam. Their maintained primary education had, it was clear, brought them both well on their educational way by the age of 11. The maintained infant or first school also frequently served as an introduction to the whole business of being a school pupil. As we saw in Chapter 5, the headmaster of a small primary school was most reluctant that parents should use his voluntary-aided school in this way for two years, then take the children off to the private sector when all the hard work of socialising into the pupil role had been done, and before they had begun to make a real contribution to the communal life of the school. But this was just what happened (in different schools) with Brian Quex and Claudia Lennox and seemed likely to happen to Caroline Tanner and Rex Henry when they reached the age of 7.

Another purpose served by the maintained and aided primary schools was in enabling the children to make local friends, to feel part of their neighbourhood community, before moving off to something rather different in the way of education from their classmates. Mrs Fellowes, Mrs Lennox and Mrs Quex were all conscious that they had been glad for their children to have this experience in their early years. But maintaining the link with neighbourhood children was not always easy. Alexander Lennox still had one close friend from his maintained school-days, and Mrs Lennox felt embarrassed when their friend sometimes came with her in the car to pick up Alexander from his preparatory school. The contrast between the schooling amenities each boy was now experiencing was so marked.

In several ways the maintained sector served a purpose for those children who then passed from it to the coexisting private sector. The school also served as the ever-available recipient of those children who came and went, in the gaps between other forms of education. Bridget, Neville and Grahame Ewell, also Glenda Irwin, were all short-term pupils at maintained schools during their parents' periods of leave in the UK.

Coexistence of the maintained with the private sector also meant that for some members of families where most of the children went to fee-paying schools there was still somewhere for the less studious or school-orientated children of the family to go throughout their schooling years. Children who did not pass the entrance exams for independent schools or had not wished to make the transfer to a different school could stay in maintained education until 16 or 18 at no cost to their parents. The maintained schools were also there to receive all those young people who, because of changed family circumstances or because the independent sector no longer seemed suited to their needs, finished out their schooling years in local authority schools.

The coexistence of two sectors of education means then, for parents, an extension of choice spanning both the maintained, aided and the many kinds of independent schools, with their varied *raisons d'être*. This extended choice is available to those who have passed what is for them the threshold of affordability of fee-paying education and are in a position to take it or leave it as they think best, and also those families who, for one reason or another, can tap into sources of public funding for payment of private school fees.

As well as an extension of choice, the coexistence of public and private education means that all families have a fall-back set of schools, the local-authority schools, which they are entitled to use at any time for any of their children between the ages of 5 and 16 and usually on to 18. Families may not always be able to place their child in a particular school, but for every child there will always be a free-to-the-user school place somewhere in the area.

The fact that a certain range of schools exists in both sectors of education, and that all parents have access to some of them (the public-sector schools) and some parents have access to all of them (those parents who can raise the fees for private-sector schools) does not necessarily mean that the schools which exist in either sector are exactly the kind of schools that parents want for their children. Choice of school is one parental 'right' which is exercised in families' use of the two sectors of education. But what of the parental 'right' to influence, govern or control schools where their children are pupils? Educational coexistence gave parents scope for the exercise of three options.

Exit, voice and loyalty

The options of exit, voice and loyalty were first conceptualised and discussed by Hirschman (1970) as responses to decline in firms, organisations and states. As a mode of analysis these concepts also have applicability, as Hirschman points out, to 'a wide range of social, political and indeed moral phenomena'. In our own study they provide a form of analysis for parents' dealings with their children's schools, in both sectors of education.

The notion of exit as a way of influencing organisations is sometimes also referred to as 'voting with the feet'. The shareholder who sells out, the member who resigns, the employee who quits, the customer who takes his business elsewhere all convey the message, implicit if not explicit, that the enterprise, association or company no longer has their support nor, possibly, their confidence. The parent who takes his or her child away from a school, may be conveying a similar message.[5]

An alternative way of conveying the same message is, however, to use voice. The expression of an opinion, a complaint, a suggestion for change, participation in a petition or collective protest all come under the heading of 'voice'.

The third option of 'Loyalty' is less easy to express in a few words. Hirschman defines it, in circular fashion, as 'that special attachment to an organisation known as "Loyalty"'. As a rule, he adds, 'loyalty holds exit at bay and activates voice' (Hirschman 1970, p. 78). In other words, those who are reluctant to leave an organisation or system because of their attachment to it, are more likely to try to influence that organisation to rectify errors and improve performance. Loyalty is not, however, in all cases the 'good guy' option; unwilling loyalty may be forced on an individual because the initial barriers to entry were so costly to overcome, while the penalties for exit are so considerable that 'sticking it out' is the only option.

In applying these concepts of exit, voice and loyalty to the behaviour of twenty-five families it is clear that all the families had made some use of the exit option. At least some of the children in each family had changed sector in the course of their education. For example, although Norman Irwin and Reah Slieman had all their education in the maintained sector, their siblings were educated in both maintained and independent schools. And while Denzil Norland and Rebecca Norland were being educated in the independent and maintained sectors, respectively, their elder brother and sister, Peregrine and Laura, had moved across the sectors at the age of 9.

Between them the seventy-two children in the sample made no less than sixty-four exits from one sector to another. Only fifteen of these were clearly due to changes in family circumstances (working abroad, moving house, loss of income following divorce, etc.); the rest were indications of dissatisfaction, loss of confidence, or the criticism implicit in the belief that what the other sector had to offer was to be preferred. Cross-sectoral exits were in both directions, but in this sample group of families moves from the maintained to the independent sector were three times as frequent as moves from the independent to the maintained sector.[6]

Given that these families had, for one reason or another, been able to use the option of exit, had this inhibited their use of voice to express any dissatisfaction or attempt to bring about change? There are a number of ways in which a parent might use voice to argue for change in a school. An individual approach could be made to a teacher or a headteacher. In the maintained sector, a parent might make a direct approach to an education officer or the director of education. The governing body could be contacted, possibly through the intermediary of a parent-governor. Alternatively, a parents' organisation, such as a parent-teacher association, might be used to convey an individual or collective dissatisfaction to the headteacher or the governors.

Several of the parents had, at some time during their children's school careers, used whichever of these channels was available to urge some kind of rethink on a maintained or independent school. They had met with varying degrees of success. Some of the more effective instances of voice were cases where the loyalty of the family to the school was also a motive for the attempt to bring about change. The Gracewell parents, for example, who thought extremely highly of the Foundation School, nevertheless battled lengthily and successfully to change a particular tradition of the school which they thought detrimental to boys' health. It was of interest that in the course of the Gracewell's campaign the board of governors offered to exempt their son from the tradition as a special case, but the Gracewells declined to accept and continued to press the principle until a policy change was agreed.

Many cases of exit had also been preceded by the attempted use of voice. Attempts to raise support from other parents, and turn an individual complaint into a collective pressure for change were, however, rarely referred to. Mrs Peel had found from experience that although fellow parents might agree in private that a change was needed, the parent who actually drew the school's attention to this could find that supporting voices were silent. Mrs Fellowes, whose daughter Kim was in oversized classes at primary school, suggested to a parent–governor that there should be a campaign to limit intake numbers, which she understood other local schools were already doing. The governor 'read her a lecture on county policy and told her there was nothing she could do about it'. Mrs Fellowes could arouse no supporting interest from other parents and did not pursue the matter further. After Kim left the school (for a reason not directly associated with class size) the teacher/pupil ratio at the school deteriorated even further and parents began to be more active in protest.

Although the exit, voice and loyalty paradigm was clearly as applicable to schools as to other organisations, there were a number of special features which inhibited the use of parental voice. The chief of these in parents' terms was the vulnerability of 'the child in the middle'. If the use of voice was not responded to by the school as a constructive and acceptable criticism, any resentment felt by teacher or headteacher might rebound on the child. Mrs Ordwell considered that an active parent should be subtle rather than radical: 'If you are radical they might take it out on the child.' Mrs Henry, a practising teacher, said, 'Any attempts I have made as a parent to change things at schools have always come back on the child, and now I have learnt not to do it.'

All the parents were asked whether they had ever, as a parent, tried to change anything at any of the schools either for their own or other people's children. The reaction of some teacher-parents to this question was sufficiently sharp to give support to the notion of teacher 'touchiness'. For one teacher-parent, the 'slings and arrows of outraged parents' were all too familiar for him to consider launching any such arrows himself. Another teacher-parent also considered that professional solidarity ruled out any attempt to bring pressure to bear on an individual teacher. He had been urged by a headteacher to contact the education department regarding his dissatisfaction with a particular teacher's methods of working, so that his complaint could be added to those already recorded by other parents. He declined to do this: 'As a teacher I couldn't do that to a colleague.' Rather than encourage a parent to make a formal complaint, it would, he felt, have been more professional for the headteacher to have 'covered up' for the inadequate teacher and made sure he taught a different set of boys next year: 'Every school has teachers who shouldn't be there.' Mrs Henry included herself in the admission that teachers were hypersensitive to criticism. They were, she felt, in a vulnerable position compared with other professionals because their clients were so numerous: 'Out of thirty children you were bound to be vulnerable regarding at least 5 of them.'

Another aspect of schooling which discouraged the use of voice to bring about change was the existence of natural breaks in education. If the child was soon to move on to the next stage of schooling, this was an opportunity to make a quiet withdrawal from the system, moving in some cases to the private sector, without going to the lengths of explaining what was wrong with the particular school. Some exits were in fact not necessarily the result of difficulties at a school but rather a dissatisfaction with the system as a whole. Both Mrs Peel and the Anthonys considered that there was no point in trying to change the whole school system. The only solution was to go elsewhere – perhaps by moving to a different education authority.

The twenty-five families, having used both public and private education for their children, were able to make comparisons between the feasibility and effectiveness of parental voice in each sector. While in principle several parents considered that those 'paying the piper should be able to call the tune', in practice parents did not consider that independent schools were markedly more ready than public-sector schools to accept proposals for change. Mr and Mrs Yalt said that at their son's preparatory school, an institution which had their warm approval, parental co-operation had been enlisted to get things done that the headmaster wanted, but 'any attempt by parents to interfere with the academic standards of the school would certainly not have been tolerated'. The Irwins did not consider that parents had more 'clout' in the private sector because they were paying. If a private school had a policy on something that policy would prevail, and the children would have to fit into it.

Nevertheless, some of the parents had found that expressions of parental opinion or anxiety and parents' enquiries about their own children's progress were more willingly received and responded to in the independent schools. Teachers in these schools gave their own home telephone numbers to parents of their pupils and were prepared to be contacted there. While many teachers in maintained schools gave the impression they did not like children, teachers in the independent sector were still smiling at the end of a long day and willing to talk to parents, in the experience of some families. Mrs Cardew considered that teachers in the private sector seemed to appreciate parental interest and to be more approachable, and parents who paid fees felt more entitled to ask for appointments. In the state sector, she contended, teachers appeared to take the view that the education of children was their business only. They held back from telling parents things so as to keep in control through superior information. Mrs Peel shared the view that parents encountered a more friendly, relaxed and open attitude from teachers at independent schools: 'The teachers there will tell you the truth – not just the good.'

Mrs Zaro considered that willingness to accept parental enquiry was one of the main differences between the public and the private sectors: 'Some state schools are like doctors' surgeries – you feel people are doing a big favour in talking to you.'[7] The highest praise she could give to the maintained primary school which her daughter now attended was that it was 'in many ways like a private school. The teachers there were just as caring of the individual child as if they thought you might take the child away.'

All the parents in the sample had used exit in what they saw as the best interests of their children's education. Most had also made some use of voice and, as we have seen, had in some (but not all) cases found a greater willingness to acknowledge the existence of a parental viewpoint in the independent schools. Was loyalty ruled out for parents who took such an active interest in their children's education, to the extent of exercising choice not only between schools but also between sectors? In fact, loyalty in all the forms envisaged by Hirschman was exemplified by one or another family at some stage in their children's schooling.

Several families had started out with the principled belief that parents should always back a school and show solidarity with teachers in the face of childish complaints. Cumulative circumstances had sometimes caused them to abandon this position, but once a difficult decision had been made to move the child, the propensity reasserted itself to show commitment to the school their child now attended. Mr and Mrs Winnicott said that rather than 'nitpick about petty school issues', like some other parents, they preferred to 'register our confidence in the school in which we have placed our sons'. Paying for education seemed in some instances positively to encourage attachment to a school. Some parents, however, were equally loyal to maintained schools. The Barnetts, whose elder sons had been to a direct-grant school and whose younger sons were educated in the maintained sector, thought that only under the most extreme and unusual circumstances would they do anything other than stick with and support a school once a child was a pupil there. It would, they felt, be impossible to anticipate how a child would perform in a different environment. Only if a child was desperately unhappy and asked to leave would a move be contemplated.

For some parents who had made the move to the private sector, loyalty in the sense of sticking with the decision once made now seemed the only feasible option. In line with Hirschman's thesis, such parents explained that since entry barriers to the school were high it would be unwise subsequently to use voice and foolish to use the option of exit. With so many children competing to get places at the school, you would not be missed. Mrs Quex was present at a social gathering at her son's preparatory school when another parent complained about the drawbacks of Saturday morning school. The following day that parent received a letter from the headteacher saying if she did not like the school's arrangements she had better remove her child.

There was also some feeling that once into the private sector one must play the game their way since penalties for exit might also be high. For instance, if using a preparatory school it could be unwise to consider moving the child before the age of 13. A younger child left behind at the school might well be penalised if an older brother made a premature exit from the school at 11 years old.

Hirschman's purpose in deploying the concepts of exit, voice and loyalty was to show the ways in which organisations might be prevailed on to improve poor performance. Parents able to contemplate the use of either sector of education certainly exercise all the available options. Whether their choices do anything to improve performance in either sector will depend on future policies regarding the coexistence of the two sectors of education.

TEN

Private Schools and State Schools: Two Systems or One?

My exploratory study of what the coexistence of public and private education means for providers and users in the 1980s has covered a good deal of ground. I have looked at the relevance of the independent sector for the operations of local education authorities and shown something of what the coexistence of the maintained sector means for headteachers of independent schools. I have also examined the ways in which some families take account and make use of the coexistence of public and private education.

What light do my findings throw on Baroness Young's assertion that the public and private sectors together make up one system of education?[1] Certainly, it is clear that the two sectors do not exist in isolation. As things stand at present, the removal of private education would be an amputation suffered by providers and users of the maintained sector rather than a business-like rationalisation of provision. But the organic metaphor cannot be taken too far. If the present functions of independent schools become more clearly understood, it may be possible for maintained education to take on those functions – to grow another limb, so to speak. Before turning to the question of possible future development, some of the issues raised by my study will be briefly reviewed.

Do the independent schools make up a coherent 'private sector' of education?

The review in Chapter 1 of policy changes over fifty years showed that because of the direct-grant arrangement, and the prominence of the famous schools (which I have, where possible, avoided calling public schools), the impression was conveyed that fee-paying schools were a broadly homogeneous group of high-calibre selective secondary schools, differentiated by a pecking order of exclusivity, but similar in aims and style. These schools were single-sex in their pupil populations, and since the stereotype of their product was the public-school boy or man, it was evident which sex, in the popular mind, was seen as being educated in these schools.

However, my exploratory research, even within a limited geographical area, has shown that independent schools are not a homogeneous group of institutions working in collaboration – however loosely linked – to provide an alternative 'sector' of education. Those schools most similar in their aims and pupil populations were at least as much in competition with one another as with the maintained sector. For other schools like Culinara, and even more the Philosopher's School, being independent meant being more or less unique, having little or no systematic contact with other independent institutions. Educational pathways for pupils at fee-paying schools, and stages of transfer, were far from clear-cut in many cases. For most of the head-teachers, the *raison d'être* of their schools was not to be a staging post on a traditional journey through a system of independent education, but to provide a distinctive educational experience from which boys or girls – or boys *and* girls, for several of the schools were co-educational – would move off in a multiplicity of directions. That these distinctive educational experiences were just what some parents were seeking for their children, was a fact not generally appreciated in the local authorities' education departments. Here the attitude taken was that parents must, of course, be allowed to make their own decisions about their children's education, but that it was a pity they were ill equipped to take such decisions. The possibility exists, however, that parents knew more than the local education authority about the range of educational experiences available in independent schools.

Are private schools and state schools complementary or in competition with each other?

If private schooling were more homogeneous, this question would be easier to debate in a clear-cut even if not a conclusive way. But independent schools, as I have pointed out, are not all academically selective secondary schools. Perhaps the most accurate summary of the relationship of private schools and state schools in the 1980s is that they are to a considerable extent complementary in their aims and operations, but they are undoubtedly in competition for the raw material of pupils, the moral support of parents and, to some extent, for public finance.[2]

One of the most obvious ways in which independent schooling complements maintained education is in the provision of boarding places, especially for the children of the Services and Foreign and Commonwealth Office personnel. Even with this (relatively) stable source of boarding need, the future of the independent boarding schools can only be regarded as uncertain because of falling cohorts of school-age children, compounded by shifts in parental attitudes to the *per se* desirability of boarding education. Nevertheless, it still appears that the boarding places available in independent schools complement rather than compete with maintained-sector provision. Where maintained boarding schools exist, local authorities do not perceive it as being in their mutual interest to compete with the independent sector for boarding pupils, despite the position of considerable strength from which they could do this, compared with the ever more costly independent board-ing schools. And despite the prolonged endeavours of the Boarding Schools Association, the principal interest group, there is no sign that a national boarding policy will win the support of either the DES or the local education authorities. The localised administration of education continues to militate against a 'nation-wide' approach, especially in times of financial constraint. Hence, maintained boarding schools have been closing and are even less prominent a feature of maintained education than they have previously been. In the past, for many user groups, boarding education was synonymous with independent education. In the 1980s this perception has been becoming increasingly accurate, and it cannot be denied that private education is complementary to maintained education by virtue of its boarding schools.

Another way in which the private sector complements the maintained sector is by providing for certain forms of special educational need. The 'non-maintained' special schools at which many children with specific handi-caps, notably the blind and deaf, are educated, are charitable organisations. They are not part of the maintained sector of education, but most receive grants from central government, and fees are paid by the local authorities from which their pupils come. It is current policy to encourage these schools to operate on similar lines to local-authority schools as far as school govern-ment and various other aspects of the schools' functioning are concerned.[3] Nevertheless, the schools clearly are not part and parcel of the maintained sector, and they provide specialised forms of education with which main-tained schools are not in competition. However, like the independent boarding schools, the non-maintained special schools do not face a cloudless future. Developments in health care and medical practice have in some cases reduced the populations of children with the specific handicaps for which the schools cater. Moreover, the desirability of grouping children with a similar handicap in a specialised school is more a matter of educational debate than hitherto. The non-maintained special schools are beginning to experience a change of role, in that instead of educating children who, although handi-capped, span a range of ability, they are increasingly dealing only with severe cases of multi-handicap, children whose multiple disabilities would seem to rule them out from absorption into mainstream education.

Although their role may be changing, the non-maintained special schools will probably continue to complement rather than compete with the forms of special education available in the maintained sector. An area of special education where there has been more evident duplication and hence some competition, although till now of a muted kind, is in schools for emotionally and behaviourally disturbed (formerly known as maladjusted), children. The population of these pupils has been one for which the fee-paying sector has made extensive provision in a plethora of small schools, and local education authorities have made considerable use of these schools for children with this kind of special educational need. But many authorities do maintain special schools for this type of pupil, and if the numbers concerned fall in proportion with overall pupil rolls, it is likely that the independent schools for emotionally and behaviourally disturbed (EBD) children will have to compete more actively for pupils, as the overspill from suitable maintained special schools becomes smaller. Moreover, the desire to reduce out-of-county expenditure may encourage local authorities to extend or reorganise their own provision for EBD pupils.[4]

The education of dyslexic pupils is another area where patterns of coexistence between public and private education may change. Dyslexia pressure-group activity has shown a tendency to splinter in its dealings with independent schools and the local education authorities. While the overall aim has been to ensure official recognition of dyslexia as a specific learning difficulty rather than a general manifestation of slow learning capacity, activity to ensure that these special educational needs can be met seems likely to increase competition between public and private education. A number of independent schools now cater specifically (although not always exclusively) for dyslexic pupils, and the recent legal judgement[5] may influence more local authorities to pay the fees of 'statemented' pupils at such independent schools. But at the same time the maintained sector may, through specialised in-service training, be increasing its capacity to cope with children with the specific learning difficulty of dyslexia, without recourse to fee-paying schools.

Public funds, whether from the Ministry of Defence, the Department of Education and Science, or via local education authorities, are expended on many of the complementary places which independent schools provide to meet boarding and special educational need which for one reason or another cannot be handled through maintained-sector provision. A much smaller number of places is paid for by central or local government for two forms of education which the maintained sector is also rarely able to provide: the education of the child with an outstanding artistic gift, and the education of the 'vulnerable' child who needs a small school. These latter children may or may not be members of the EBD group, but usually evince the withdrawn rather than 'acting out' type of maladjustment. Some of the children whose fees were paid by local authorities at Culinara or the Philosopher's School were in this 'vulnerable' category. There are, of course, some small schools in the maintained sector of education, although not many at the secondary stage. But their size is usually the outcome of local demographic features rather than a matter of intent. Private education is complementary to the public sector in having many schools which include small size as part of their *raison d'être*. In their ability to cope with those vulnerable children deemed to need a small school, these independent schools are not in direct competition with present-day maintained schools.

As for the education of children with an artistic gift, the maintained sector has never made any sustained attempt to meet these children's needs. Two maintained schools count themselves among the 'choir' schools, but with these exceptions selective education for children with outstanding abilities in music or dance has always been provided in specialist independent schools (such as the Zenith School). It seems unlikely that public education will ever duplicate these costly forms of education, offering competition to the private schools for music and dance.

So far, this recapitulation of ways in which public and private education might be defined as complementary to or competitive with each other has referred only to forms of education where under certain circumstances public money for private-sector education might be forthcoming (boarding, special education of various kinds, the education of children with artistic gifts). A remaining and important category where direct payments are made by government to independent schools is the assisted-places scheme. Are assisted places a competitive or complementary feature of independent education *vis-à-vis* the maintained schools? There are points in support of either definition. If it is assumed that children awarded assisted places, following the 1980 Education Act, are children of high academic ability from families of limited financial means, then the scheme can be seen as competitive, for the maintained sector in its all-ability (comprehensive) schools claims to be able to meet the needs of children of every level of ability. However, in central government's terms the scheme does not explicitly set out to make academically selective secondary education available to certain children. It is described as 'enabling pupils who might otherwise not be able to do so to benefit from education at independent schools'.[6] The 'benefit' appears to lie in the independence of the school and is not linked to any requirement that the school shall provide academically selective education.[7] Research being conducted by Whitty *et al.* may show whether participation agreements between the secretary of state and the independent schools offering assisted places typically include reference to academic selection, or further specify what are the 'appropriate educational standards' which the school has to maintain, if its participation agreement is not to be terminated.[8] However, since the majority of independent schools which now offer assisted places under the scheme were formerly direct-grant grammar schools, it does appear that the chief criterion of selection of pupils by the schools is likely to be level of academic ability, and that the schools are therefore potentially in competition for a particular segment of pupils who would otherwise be educated in all-ability schools, or one of the few grammar schools which remain in the maintained sector. But some interested parties would claim that the great majority of comprehensive schools are not able fully to meet the educational needs of the most academically able, so that the independent schools, in catering for such children, are supplementing rather than competing with maintained education.[9]

The cases reviewed above where public money is spent on independent schooling are important, but they are only a small percentage of the school places for which fees are paid. For the most part it is parents, not government departments or local education authorities, who decide if it is essential, or desirable, to pay fees for a child to attend an independent school rather than take up a place at a local maintained school, which is free of direct cost to the parent.[10] Are parents who choose between the two sectors of education doing so on the basis that public and private education are complementary, with discrete and distinctive aims and outcomes, but combining to form a single wide-ranging system of education? Or do they see the independent and maintained sectors as two systems in competition with one another, striving to achieve the same ends but with apparently varying degrees of success?

My study of twenty-five families can use their experience to shed light on these questions. The themes of movement from the public to the private sector discussed in Chapters 7 and 8 illustrate some of the ways in which the panoply of public and private education is perceived by parents. For those parents who had experience of the direct-grant scheme, and for whom the 'direct-grant effect' was a factor influencing educational choices for their children, these schools represented a standard of excellence beyond anything available in the maintained sector, but with which the public sector was in competition in that the maintained grammar schools and the direct-grant schools had similar aims. After 1975, for some parents the 'ex-direct-grant schools' still represented the same desirable standard of excellence, and one to which in their view the maintained sector no longer aspired. In that sense, the two sectors had ceased to compete, having differing aims.

A second theme was of parents who had been satisfied customers of the maintained grammar schools, either for themselves or for their children, and who now concluded that 'more of the same' was only available in the private sector. These families had either not been aware of, or had disregarded, the competition offered by direct-grant or other fee-paying grammar schools when the maintained grammar schools existed. The fee-paying schools only came into focus for these families when maintained selective secondary education was wound up.

Both these themes of movement were influenced by living memory of a form of education no longer available on the same terms but, in these families' estimation, still to be desired. Neither the complementary nor the competitive paradigm fully fits their decision-making. Their analysis was based on a historical residue. It is reasonable to suppose that the frames of reference of future parents, who have grown up since 1975, will not be influenced by memories of direct-grant or maintained grammar schools, and will instead take account of their own (probably comprehensive) secondary education in appraising what is desirable and feasible for their children's schooling. But there may, of course, be new types of school available by the time individuals born in the 1970s are making decisions as parents of school-age children.

A third theme of movement was by 'natural' users of the private sector for whom the state system had served as a temporary substitute. This theme has more clear-cut competitive features. Here it was the maintained sector which had been seen by some parents as competing with the private sector, in the sense that it offered a feasible alternative educational route rather than one that was out of the question. Since the decision was subsequently made that satisfactory education did after all have to be paid for, it is evident that the maintained sector was not, in the longer term, a successful competitor for these parents' support. But for a while at least these families had appraised the maintained and independent schools as competing providers of much the same educational experience.

Turning to the families who were aspiring users of the private sector because it was 'bound to be better', these families too were using a competition model, a competition in which the private sector was, for them, in a position to win hands down. This was not because the independent schools were seen as educating a different type or class of child. Most of the parents who took the 'bound to be better' view of private education pointed out that in a suburban area the families who used private schools and state schools were indistinguishable and frequently interchanging. But the financial contract between home and school encouraged teachers to mobilise the potential of each and every child, and made the teacher–parent relationship a more equal partnership where both saw each other as legitimately in the business of seeking the child's advancement. In competing with maintained schools to educate children, the schools where fees were paid therefore drew on resources of teacher and parent commitment and motivation which were simply not present in 'free' education, in these parents' view.

In other cases of movement from the public to the private sector of education, both the complementary and the competitive paradigms seemed inadequate as an explanation of the user's view of educational coexistence. These were cases of families alienated by their contemporary experience of state primary or secondary education and who took the decision to move their children from maintained to independent schools. Parental choice of school has been much debated as a theoretical notion. In these cases we see it at work in practice. These parents all had clear expectations of what maintained education, whether at the primary or secondary stage, should be able to provide for their child. They did not all have the same expectations, and they recognised that other parents might not want the same thing as themselves. They therefore did not anticipate or require that each maintained school should be like any other maintained primary or secondary school.

What they did hope for was to identify a school whose style and aims appeared to match their own expectations and their child's needs, to be able to get a place for their child at that school, and to find that the school was managed in a way that enabled its aims to be systematically furthered. This expectation of having access to an identifiable and coherent institution was not fulfilled by their experience in maintained education in the 1980s, and they turned to private education to see if their expectations could be matched there.

From these parents' point of view it was not adequate to describe public and private education as two systems having the same aims which each strove to fulfil better than the other (the competitive paradigm), nor to see private schools and state schools as having different aims which they pursued in non-competitive coexistence as a single system of education (the complementary paradigm). They expected schools within the maintained sector to have a variety of aims and that some schools but not others would suit their child and themselves. Frequently, they had identified such a maintained school but had not been able to arrange for their child to attend it. In other cases they had got a place for their child at a maintained school whose aims and apparent style they supported, only to find that the school was not run as a coherent whole, and its philosophies and practice varied from classroom to classroom. In moving their child to an independent school, most of these families had found satisfaction, largely because each school stated clearly what it was set up to do and did it singlemindedly. In other words, the parents recognised the *raison d'être* of the individual independent school and saw it being fulfilled. As for access to the school of choice, this was much more in the parents' hands, because of the fee-paying factor, than it was in the maintained sector.[11]

The remaining themes of pupil movement from the public to the private sector were where families needed or wanted boarding education for their children or saw themselves as dealing with a 'problem' child. Some of the reasons why boarding education and private education were often seen as synonymous have already been discussed. Parents who urgently needed boarding education for their children immediately approached the private sector, which they or their advisers perceived as comprising the schools where boarding education was readily available (a feature which complemented the non-residential maintained sector).

In a few cases parents sent their children to independent schools where boarding was part of the 'package' rather than a positive feature of choice, and these were cases which were similar to the 'clear expectations, *raison d'être* seeking' group previously described. Families looking for a school to benefit a problem child were also looking for a particular style of school rather than a form of education which the sectors might be competing to provide or which might be available in one sector and not the other. They wanted a school which particularly set out to be responsive to the needs of individual children.

In some cases the child's problems were perceived as allied to 'giftedness' or to consist of the need for encouragement, the 'faith that it matters',[12] which had to be imparted to an able but lazy child. These parents' experience that, in the event, their child's problems abated in an independent rather than a maintained school may imply that recognising and responding to children of high ability was not an ambition of maintained schools and that the independent schools supplemented the maintained sector by taking on these children. In practice, these parents *had* found that the maintained sector seemed content to let the independent schools take on board the problems as well as the rewards of teaching children of high ability.[13] But on the whole it seemed that for parents of 'problem' children the quest was for a school geared to individuality rather than a school specifically set up to nurture the able. They did not see why this *raison d'être* of responsiveness should be the prerogative of independent schools, but in practice they found it to be so.

In examining the case histories of twenty-five families who have moved back and forth between private schools and state schools, one thing has become clear. Although the independent schools may still be educating only about 6 per cent of the school-age population, it is not always the same individuals whose heads are counted. Many more than 6 per cent of the pupil population experience independent schooling at some time during their education. Whether their families see private schools and state schools as two systems or one, they take both sectors into account when making educational plans for their children.

From the point of view of parents, would education vouchers be a good thing?

Voucher schemes take many potential forms. One suggestion, which has been seriously discussed at some levels,[14] is that parents might be given a voucher for each child, exchangeable for a financially costed amount of education at the school of their choice, whether maintained or independent. Would parents welcome this?

My research has shown that there are already some parents who, without the benefit of a voucher, nevertheless operate in just the way that this 'cross-sector' type of voucher scheme envisages. They know what they want by way of education for a particular child, they try to find out where such education is available – and are prepared to appraise a wide range of institutions in the process – and having decided on a school, put their best endeavours to ensuring that their application matches the requirements of the school's admission policy. Voucher in hand, their task would be easier, especially since any cross-sector voucher scheme would necessarily diminish the power of the local-education authority to superimpose 'efficient use of resources' requirements[15] on parental choice between schools in the maintained sector. For the parents who took part in the research, education vouchers would undoubtedly have been a good thing – and would have helped to allay any fears that in sending different members of the family to different schools they were somehow being unfair in that some schooling was paid for directly by the family and some by the state. Are there other parents who would feel able to make good use of education vouchers?

I have not claimed that parents who responded to my newspaper request for help were necessarily typical of other parents. Can it perhaps be contended that they were grossly *untypical*? Is it possible that my research took place in the only part of the country where parents take any interest in what schools their children attend and that, within that geographical area, my invitation caught the eye of the few dozen families who not only cared which schools their children attended but were prepared to take active steps to see that their children were accepted by the preferred school, whether in the public or the private sector of education? It is my contention that there was nothing unique about the twenty-five families I interviewed (or the other sixty families who replied to the advertisement). They were merely prime examples of the 'parent as consumer of educational provision' – a role which all parents play during their child's compulsory schooling years and which some take up with enthusiasm from the nursery stage. Parents in the research had reached the threshold of affordability which enabled them to consider some fee-paying schools, so that their parental choice of school spanned both public and private education. But even before this, when looking only at maintained schools, they had tried hard to exercise effective choice. These parents' accounts of educational discussions and exchanges of information with friends, neighbours and the parents of their children's school fellows, in a wide range of neighbourhoods and schools, made it clear that there were others who shared their wish to bring parental judgment to bear on the type of schooling their children should receive. Where only maintained education was in question, there were many examples given of frustrated parental choice.

In speculating about the possible attitudes to educational choice of a whole nation of parents with school-age children, one can envisage a nucleus of activists for whom a voucher would be an additional asset in a choice activity on which they would in any case embark; also a wider circle of parents for whom it would enlarge the sphere over which their appraisal presently ranged (enabling them, in the case of a cross-sector voucher, to consider schools in the private sector); even more parents who had tried to exercise choice within the maintained sector but had been frustrated by administrative or procedural impediments; still more who had never actively tried to exercise choice because they were sure it wouldn't work, and some who had never thought about it, accepting what appeared to be the norm for the locality and thinking themselves 'lucky' or 'unlucky' as the case might be. Such parents might need counselling to help them exercise parental choice. Such counselling is already available, on an entrepreneurial basis, from alert educational cognoscenti like Mrs Henry.[16] In the event of a nation-wide voucher scheme, there could well be a need for the kind of advisory service for parents choosing schools which is already available to Service parents through the Service Children's Education Authority.

ELEVEN

Problems and Prospects

Nothing stands still in education. The central/local division of powers means that even if 'no change', for reasons of political expediency or parliamentary timetabling, is the policy of a ruling central administration, local authorities can initiate policy changes which entail decisive shifts and may bring latent conflict rapidly into the open.

Conflicts inherent in the status quo of educational coexistence

In Morrowshire and Robart, educational coexistence was in a state of political quiescence. Private schools and maintained schools existed alongside one another without open rivalry, and some low-profile inter-school exchanges and co-operation even took place on a strictly informal basis.[1] Robart education authority's Saturday Music School was attended by children from both sectors of education. And in cases where parents moved their children from one sector to another, sometimes with the help of authority funding, these occurrences were defined as personal choices, possibly indicative of private troubles, but not constituting a public issue. In other authorities, however, the potential conflict of interest inherent in the coexistence of public and private education was more to the fore. The controversy about Nottinghamshire's swimming pools was a case in point.

The Nottinghamshire controversy began in 1984, when the education committee took a decision to stop independent-school pupils from using council facilities, on the grounds that the authority needed to maximise the opportunities available to maintained pupils. The facilities in question included playing fields, Saturday morning classes, including music schools and sessions, and was to be extended to swimming pools. Immediate responses from individuals and interest groups affiliated to independent schools included a high-court injunction, intended to be followed by full judicial review; a request to the secretary of state to exercise his powers under Sections 68 and 99 of the 1944 Act to direct the local authority to rescind its 'unreasonable' decision; and a complaint to the local ombudsman that the ban was 'overtly political, vindictive and unreasonably biased' and should be defined as maladministration.

None of the litigation or appeal procedures in the Nottinghamshire case was particularly effective in meeting the needs of the aggrieved. But the promptness with which these steps were taken showed the depth of feeling involved and perhaps the underlying resentment of fee-paying parents that their use of the independent sector of education gave them no remission from the rates and taxes which resource the local education authority and the maintained sector. What chiefly appears to have tempered the determination of the authority to pursue its policy of denying access to independent-school pupils was, however, the public outcry which followed the discovery that one of the independent schools concerned was a day school for autistic children. As has already been suggested, 'in special education, emotion overrides anything else'.[2] The council moved back from blanket exclusion of independent-school pupils from council facilities. Those pupils who were already taking part in music schools and orchestras were allowed to continue, and the independent schools whose pupils had special educational needs were given equal priority with maintained schools in the allocation of swimming time. A charge would, however, be made for the facility. This decision showed the residual determination of the education committee somehow to sharpen the boundary line between maintained and independent schooling. The swimming-pool fee to be paid to the authority by the independent school for the autistic children would in fact come indirectly from local-authority funds, because the fees of all twenty-eight pupils at the school were paid for by local authorities, eighteen of them by Nottinghamshire.

The case shows that there are many tensions inherent in the status quo of educational coexistence. As long as parental decisions are seen as private matters, families who can afford to do so take on school fees without demur that their rates and taxes are also supporting the public sector of education. But if any attempt is made to define privately educated children as beyond the pale as local residents, parental ire is quickly aroused. And when political groups make a move to impose sanctions on the private sector they are brought face to face with the diversity of private schooling and the fact that among those educated in fee-paying schools are disadvantaged children whose opportunities it would be politically unacceptable to attempt to curtail.

Other latent conflicts, inherent but temporarily quiescent in the status quo of educational coexistence, are concerned with religious education. There is the general question of the right of parents to send their children to a school which supports the tenets of their own religious faith. And, in the 1980s, there is the more specific demand for the inclusion of Islamic schools in the voluntary-aided arrangement – an arrangement which interest groups on the far left of the political spectrum would, by contrast, like to see phased out of the public sector of education.

One of the philosophical justifications for the continuing existence of independent alongside maintained schools, and of the so-called 'dual system' within the public sector whereby voluntary schools coexist with local authority schools, is the argument that the freedom of parents to seek a faith-linked education for their children is a fundamental human right. During 1985 and 1986 the Socialist Educational Association worked on the formulation of a future policy for integrating not only the independent schools but also the voluntary schools into a single system of state education. If this proposal for integration were to become an imminent reality, a reawakening of resistance to the secularisation of public-sector education could be expected, if not perhaps of quite the same type as that mounted by the religious lobby during the drafting of the 1944 Education Act.

The public-sector voluntary schools chiefly consist of Church of England and Roman Catholic institutions, with a few Jewish schools. In 1985 and 1986 there were signs that some changes in the relationship between local authorities and diocesan bodies would not be unwelcome,[3] but there were no positive indications that the Church of England[4] (let alone the Roman Catholic Church) was ready to consider giving up running public-sector schools altogether, despite the growing financial cost of keeping these schools going.

Gay (1985) found that as far as the independent sector was concerned, the great majority of independent schools claimed a religious affiliation. Most had been established by devout individuals or particular religious orders and did not have the backing of a diocesan infrastructure, linking them to the church as an institution. The Church of England had a very considerable stake in the independent sector. Nationally, at least 150,000 pupils were, at the time of Gay's research, educated in independent schools which claimed some association with the Church of England. At least at the secondary stage there were many more pupils in the Anglican schools in the independent sector than in the Church of England schools of the maintained sector. Nevertheless, the independent schools which claimed Anglican allegiance had no links with the synodical and decision apparatus of the Church of England. Moreover, they were almost completely independent from each other[5] and in no way constituted a privately funded religious group of schools. Their principal, and controversial, link with the church as an institution was via the ordained ministry. The schools had over time, contributed massively though decreasingly to clergy recruitment, as ex-pupils had gone forward for ordination. The schools continued to employ a considerable number of ordained clergy as school chaplains, and their governing bodies were studded with bishops. The boarding schools were also, it appeared, an acceptable environment for many clergy children and made it possible for ministers to work in inner-city areas without involving their own children in inner-city problems.[6]

Gay pointed out that the Church of England had no system of religious accreditation or approved list of independent schools. If the independent schools were in future to find their 'integration' coerced by attempts to erode their financial position as educational charities, some of them would have a strong case for continuing as religious charities. They might well turn to the church for support on these grounds, in which case the Church of England would be forced to re-examine the ambiguities of its own attitude to educational coexistence.

The accreditation role for the growing number of religious independent schools in the United Kingdom falls at present not to the religious bodies concerned but to HMI, which has a role in the registration of each and every school. The new independent schools are in most cases not additions to the existing number of Anglican or Roman Catholic schools. Some are promoted by Christian minority groups[7] or minority Jewish sects.[8] Others are for Muslim children.

By the mid-1980s the United Kingdom population included over 1·5 million Muslims, some of whose children attended the twenty or so fee-paying Muslim schools which had been established. Large numbers of Muslim children were, however, being educated in maintained schools, not always in accordance with the wishes of their parents, since the Islamic faith incorporates a number of required observances, including practices for the protection of girls. In some areas of high Muslim concentration, however, local authorities reported changes in schools made as concession to Islamic values.[9] Nevertheless some Muslim parents began to campaign for voluntary-aided Muslim schools. They claimed that the only reason these had not always been available, like Anglican, Catholic and Jewish schools, was that at the time of the 1944 Act there was no substantial Muslim community in Britain. In 1983 a Muslim parents' association in Bradford sought voluntary-aided status for five schools. Their application was rejected, in part because of the likelihood that such schools would have wholly Asian pupil populations,[10] an educational separation which the Swann report on multi-ethnic education had not commended.[11] A subsequent attempt to set up a voluntary-aided Muslim school was made by a minority sect – contested as non-Muslim by the orthodox Muslim community – and this attempt also foundered. But in 1985 Brent Council recommended to the secretary of state that an Islamic private school should become the first Muslim voluntary-aided school in the country.

In the United Kingdom the religious issue and questions of educational coexistence have not been prominently interwoven, but the connection and the potential conflicts are there. If and when political controversy reheats about the future roles of the independent, the voluntary and the local-authority schools in the education system, religious arguments will increasingly be brought into play.

What is the future of educational coexistence?

When this enquiry into contemporary patterns of educational coexistence began, there appeared to be three main possibilities for the future: a continuation of the status quo; the abolition of private education; the aggregation of public and private education into a single 'market' where consumer choice would be sovereign. My research set out to explore what the 'status quo' in the co-existence of private schools and state schools actually implied for providers and users. But while the research has been going on, maintained education has been continuously in the limelight. All interested parties in the so-called partnership of maintained education have been at odds with one another and dissatisfied with the education service which is their joint concern.

The points at issue could scarcely be more fundamental: the future of central–local relations in the provision of education; the professional standing and remuneration of teachers (and the managerial relationship between headteachers and teachers); the accountability of teachers both as individual professionals and as members of unionised collectives; the rights of consumers (parents and pupils) faced with a service in disarray; the appropriate programme for public compulsory education at a time of high unemployment and technological change.

To set out all the strands of argument regarding these issues would need a separate book – and no doubt several such books are currently being written. Many of the controversies, in particular the debates about central–local relations in education, and about the appropriate substance of public education, are of long standing. The fact that all the controversies are simultaneously and manifestly unresolved may generate the political will to do something about them. Suggestions have been coming forth piecemeal for new institutions (such as 'crown' schools, 'new direct-grant' schools and 'corporation' schools), new forms of professional contract, new incentives for pupils to continue their education, new opportunities for parental choice and influence. As always, the central argument is about new allocations of government funding. In 1986 public-sector education shows no sign of settling back into makeshift compromise and obscurity, but a pay package with commitment to future measures of reform may shelve some of the more awkward controversies until electoral manifestos are produced.

I have claimed that how people feel about private education is always a function of how they feel about public education.[12] What effect is the present upheaval in public education likely to have on the future of private education? It seems unlikely that there is still sufficient political mileage in the abolition of private education for the Labour Party to retain this as a tenet of future education policy. When the education of the 94 per cent of children in the public sector is in turmoil there is little incentive to mount a campaign for the compulsory enrolment of the residual 6 per cent, at present educated outside the maintained system. But the private schools would almost certainly have to fend for themselves, without benefit of 'subsidies' or of assisted places, under any future Labour administration, if only in order to demonstrate that all available resources were being focused on collective provision.

What is the likelihood of a continuation of the status quo? Earlier discussion in this chapter showed that there are conflicts inherent even in the status quo of educational coexistence. But at least until the next general election the private schools seem well placed to stand by and pick up survivors able to escape from the foundering ship of maintained education. My research has shown that the private schools have some sort of a complementary role to play in any case, as a supplement to maintained provision, and that some parents also judge the private schools as useful adjuncts to the maintained sector, worth investing in for one child if not all children in the family, or for part of the educational process if not its whole. It is almost inevitable that the number of parents who take this view will increase during the interim period before something is done, and seen to be done, to resolve the controversies in maintained education. But the status quo as a post-election option seems ruled out. Any new government will be expected to do something effective about state education, and this will have consequential effects for the coexistence of private education.

In the event of a Labour or Alliance administration, the private schools could find themselves competing on far more equal, 'unsubsidised', terms with the maintained schools. And changes made by either of these administrations might be enabling state schools to emulate what have proved to be the strengths of the independent schools: individual schools developing a *raison d'être*; teachers dedicating themselves with enthusiasm to the success of the school and the development of the pupils; the self-selection of pupils following the academic path through to extended education (with others allowed to leave earlier, or offered more 'relevant' training paths). And pupils who stopped on at maintained schools after compulsory age might be motivated to progress by entitlement to maintenance allowances. Faced with a revitalised public sector, the private schools would have to look to their laurels, possibly becoming more of a *sector* and offering a clearer *system* of alternative education. Another possibility would be for the private sector to give more emphasis to its *complementary* potential, in offering all the things that get crowded out of a nation-wide system: specialised academies; schools meeting special educational need of unusual kinds; boarding education; single-sex education, faith-linked education.

But if a Conservative government, 'Thatcherite' or otherwise, were to form the next administration, the private sector could find itself with more to do than it bargained for. A modest increase in assisted places would not satisfy the expectations of those who now look to the right wing of politics to do something radical about education. At the very least the providers of private education would have to adjust to coexisting with a more diversified maintained sector, which included some new forms of institution, and they might have to enter into some new alliances in order to play a part in new hybrid institutions which were neither independent nor maintained in the presently accepted sense. Such institutions are currently a feature of the 'providers' scenario for a future Conservative government's radical revision of maintained education. But the market enthusiasts within the party might yet win the day, ostensibly on behalf of the 'users' of education. Then the independent schools, including the handful of diverse institutions which I have discussed in detail, could find themselves becoming part of a nation-wide education industry, with a potentially vastly increased market of voucher-bearing parents. Selection, already a big task for some independent schools, would become huge. Expansion and diversification would be almost inevitable. Her Majesty's Inspectorate, rather than the mutually deferential associations and Joint Council, would once again be the arbiters of what went on in the schools. Whatever the future of educational coexistence, it seems unlikely to be dull.

APPENDIX

The Research

Effective research design has been described as a compromise between the aims of the research, the resources available for its completion and the general feasibility of the area of study. (Silvey 1975). All these factors influenced the planning of the research on which this book is based.

The Leverhulme Trust made an institutional grant to the Department of Government, Brunel University, in October 1983, for a two-year study of patterns of coexistence in the public and private sectors of education. The research was designed and executed by Daphne Johnson. The aims of the research were qualitative rather than quantitative; that is to say, the intention was to explore the impressions of providers and users in both sectors of education rather than to count heads and measure frequencies of use of either sector.

The most important aspect of the research design was the decision to conduct the research as a single case study of educational coexistence in a particular geographical area. A considerable methodological literature exists which defines and describes case study research; for example, Adelman *et al.* (1984), Burgess (1982, 1984), Nisbet and Watt (1980). In exploring educational coexistence the present study most closely adheres to the definition given by Yin (1984, p. 44) of a single case study with embedded units of analysis.

Case study form was chosen for the research because such methods are particularly suitable for qualitative work which analyses the subjective accounts given by participants. Case study research design, as Yin points out, is not appropriate for measuring the incidence of phenomena. The generalisations to which case studies can give rise are analytical rather than statistical. This case study of educational coexistence was intended to identify the theoretical paradigms and illuminative concepts which are exemplified in administrative and family educational experience.

The approach to providers of education

Fieldwork for the study focused chiefly on a geographical area in the south-east of England where both sectors of education were well established and pupil movement took place between maintained and fee-paying institutions. The study was made with the co-operation of two adjacent education authorities, for which the pseudonyms of Morrowshire and Robart have been used. Interviews took place with education committee members, councillors, education officers, psychologists and advisers in both authorities. Visits were made to eighteen independent and maintained schools in the geographical area; the headteachers of these schools and the principals of three colleges of further or higher education were interviewed. Research access to each institution was individually negotiated. Within Morrowshire, apart from the contacts at county hall and visits to independent schools following particular educational traditions, research effort was concentrated on the 'Sesame' division, an area of the county with both urban and rural features. Research enquiries were also pursued with over thirty organisations and interest groups which had an involvement with independent and maintained education.

The approach to users of education

Through the local press (some twelve free circulation and commercial local newspapers) a trawl was made for parents living in or around the geographical area covered by the research and who had used both sectors of education for their children. This approach to parents, inviting their participation in the research, was made through the local press rather than through local schools so that those providing information should feel they were doing so as free-standing consumers of educational services, not as parents of a pupil at a particular school. Twenty-five of the eighty-five families who replied were interviewed at length about the circumstances of their children's education. These families were selected from the trawl chiefly because the patterns of education followed by their children appeared to exemplify a variety of approaches to educational coexistence (see Table A).

All the parents took part in several hours of semi-structured interviewing, usually on two and sometimes on three separate occasions. At the conclusion of the interviews with each family, parents answered a series of questions selected from the British Social Attitudes Survey,* giving information about occupation, politics, religion and income at the time of interview (see Jowell and Airey 1984). Chapter 7 makes reference to some of this information, and the parents' approach to their children's education is fully discussed in Chapters 7, 8 and 9. The sequence of the children's schooling in maintained and independent schools is set out in Table A. Table B shows the duration of the parents' own schooling. (These tables appear on pp. 166–9.)

*The help given by Sharon Witherspoon of Social and Community Planning Research in identifying these questions is gratefully acknowledged.

The parents' education

Twenty-six of the forty-nine parents received all their education in maintained or voluntary-aided schools. Sixteen had part of their education in the maintained and part (usually at the secondary stage) in fee-paying schools. Four of the parents had all their education in the fee-paying sector in England, and three were educated privately overseas (in India, Egypt and Ireland, respectively). Whether for reasons of family mobility, or changes of family fortune, or evacuation or other wartime disruption of education, many of the forty-six 'United Kingdom' parents had a number of changes of school during the primary or 'elementary' years.

Their secondary schooling illustrated the wide range of schools which coexisted during the parents' youth. Seven of the older parents passed the Scholarship exam and went to pre-1944 Act grammar schools, and one attended such a school as a fee-paying pupil. Two parents won scholarships to public schools as boarders, and five had free or assisted places at direct-grant schools. Five went to technical or central schools and three had an elementary education before the 1944 Act.

Six parents went to fee-paying secondary schools after the war, three of them as boarders. Twelve went to post-1944 Act free maintained or aided grammar schools, and five to secondary-modern schools. None of the parents had been a pupil at a comprehensive school. Those who were still at school in the United Kingdom in the late 1960s, when some comprehensive schools were beginning to be established, attended, respectively, a maintained grammar school, a secondary-modern school and a fee-paying convent school.

The parents' further and higher education also showed considerable variation, and not all had obtained their higher qualifications by conventional full-time study. However, the presence of many teachers in the sample meant inevitably that these parents as a whole had above-average education. Thirteen parents (seven husbands and six wives) were graduates, and six of these (one husband and five wives) also had a teaching qualification. Two of the graduate husbands had a post-graduate qualification other than for teaching. Three of the wives in the graduate group had obtained their degree as mature students. Eight further parents held a teaching certificate (one husband and seven wives). Twelve of the parents had no professional or other formal qualifications of a post-school kind. The remaining sixteen held a variety of trade, technical and professional qualifications, which demonstrated the bewildering range of available further education over the past forty years.

Notes

Chapter 1 (Politics of Coexistence, pp. 5–20)

1. The Elementary Education Act, 1870, provided for school boards, elected by local ratepayers, to set up schools in the gaps left by existing voluntary provision.
2. England and Wales are in the educational remit of the Department of Education and Science, and educational statistics are collected and published on this geographical basis; where general references are made in this book to the 'national' situation, these are the countries referred to. Educational arrangements in Scotland and Northern Ireland take distinctive forms, but the coexistence of public and private education is also to be found in these parts of the United Kingdom.
3. The notion of *no* government expenditure on education does not appear to be politically imaginable in a twentieth-century democracy.
4. The residual model can be applied to all spheres of social policy. It argues that social welfare should focus selectively on a residual and declining minority of needy groups (see Pinker 1971, p. 99). The converse 'universalist' view is that social welfare should cater for the reasonable requirements of every citizen, whatever their economic standing.
5. In 1981 and 1986 discussion documents by the Socialist Educational Association have addressed the question of the dual system of voluntary and county schools. They propose that the work and practices of both types of school be harmonised, and that over an interim period of twenty years a unified system of increasingly non-segregated schools serving increasingly pluralist communities should be voluntarily developed. Reserve powers of legislation to require this would await the outcome of harmonisation negotiations.
6. Social Democratic Party, *Education and Training*, Policy Document No. 6, London, SDP, 1983.

7. The arguments propounded in a number of publications (A. Flew, *Power to the People!* London, Centre for Policy Studies, 1983; S. R. Dennison, *Choice in Education*, London, Institute of Economic Affairs, 1984; Conservative Political Centre, *No Turning Back*, London, CPC, 1985) would logically bring an end to a system of public education. This is not openly advocated, but the free market of educational institutions and the sovereignty of parental choice are stressed.

8. The many forms of government support which are or have been available for independent education are discussed elsewhere in this book. They include charitable status, direct grants and assisted places of various kinds.

9. The United States' dedication to the principle of separation of church and state is expressed in the First Amendment to the Constitution (now part of the Bill of Rights, 1791.)

10. Voluntary schools may be 'aided, 'controlled' or 'special agreement', terms which relate to different degrees of public control and financing from the local authority and the DES. In aided schools the voluntary foundation appoints the majority of school governors. About two-thirds of voluntary schools were founded by the Church of England. The remainder are Roman Catholic, with a tiny category of Methodist and Jewish schools. The creation of Muslim voluntary-aided schools is under debate.

11. See, for example, Tawney (1931), Crosland (1964, Ch. 10), Halsey *et al.* (1980). More recently, writers who have reiterated the class reproduction function of the private sector of education include Fox (1985, Ch. 1) and Salter and Tapper (1985, Ch. 3).

12. The full title was 'The National Society for Promoting the Education of the Poor in the Principles of the Established Church'. The Nonconformist society was the British and Foreign School Society.

13. This résumé ignores the small private schools for the lower middle and upper working class which overlapped with the free elementary schools around the turn of the nineteenth and twentieth centuries. Burnett (1982) makes brief reference to these. Forerunners of these private schools were the 'dames schools' of the eighteenth and nineteenth centuries, where some children from families of very moderate means received a basic educational grounding for a few pence a week. The thesis that before the advent of public education the working population was far from universally unlettered is explored by West (1975).

14. A very few pupils, among those who did not pass (or take) the Scholarship, had a second chance at 13 when a further competitive examination gave access in some areas to technical, art and commercial schools in the maintained sector.

15. See Gosden (1976) and Kogan (1978, p. 25). Kogan suggests that the Forces vote was a new factor in the 1945 election, which brought Labour to power to carry through many of the social reforms planned under a coalition government during the war years. The extent to which the Army Bureau of Current Affairs contributed to the further education, and in particular the political education, of those servicemen who had

hitherto received only elementary schooling, is a topic of its own which cannot be explored here.

16. The health authorities were given responsibility for the local billeting of evacuated children.

17. In the 1980s there has been a revival of interest in the personal experiences of those who lived through the Second World War. Radio programmes (e.g. *Home from Home*, a documentary by David Wade, BBC, August 1985) and books (e.g. C. Jackson, *Who Will Take Our children?* London, Methuen, 1985) have focused on evacuation. A wider range of wartime reminiscence is provided by Croall (1987).

18. Board of Education, *Educational Reconstruction*, London, HMSO, 1943, Cmnd. 6458.

19. The Fleming Committee was the Committee on Public Schools, under the chairmanship of the Hon. Lord Fleming, appointed by the president of the Board of Education in July 1942. The Fleming report, *The Public Schools and the General Educational System*, was published on behalf of the Board of Education by HMSO in 1944.

20. Fleming Report, para. 4.

21. Scheme A proposed a scheme of association for the public schools somewhat similar to that of the direct-grant schools. Scheme B envisaged a system of bursaries for individual pupils from maintained schools who would become boarders at a public school from the age of 13, or at an appropriate preparatory school from the age of 11. A few such bursaries were awarded, and the experiences of a Fleming Report pupil were dramatised in Warren Chetham-Strodes' play *The Guinea Pig*, 1946, London, S. Low, Marston & Co. Ltd.

22. This expression was used by Mrs Dare, one of the parents contributing to the research.

23. *Second Report of the Public Schools Commission*, London, HMSO, 1970, Vol. 1, para. 172.

24. See, for example, Floud *et al.* (1956), Fraser (1959) and Jackson and Marsden (1963).

25. Fleming Report, paras. 145–7.

26. *First Report of the Public Schools Commission*, London, HMSO, 1968., Vol. 2, App. 8.

27. A notable exception to these accounts is Kogan's *The Politics of Educational Change*, London, Fontana, 1978 which conveys the swings of policy and opinion without overwhelming the non-specialist reader with the minutiae of administrative documentation.

28. *First Report of The Public Schools Commission*, Vol. 1, Terms of Reference, Objective (b).

29. *Ibid.*, Note of Dissent, para. 9.

30. *Ibid.*, para. 392.

31. Fleming Report, para. 123.

32. Ministry of Education, *Report of the Working Party on Assistance with the Cost of Boarding Education* (Martin Report), London, HMSO, 1960. Guidelines for boarding need put forward in the report are reproduced in Chapter 3.

33. *First Report of the Public Schools Commission*, Vol. 1. Note of Reservation, para 8.
34. *Ibid.*, para. 302.
35. *Ibid.*, para. 101.
36. Central Advisory Council for Education, *Children and Their Primary Schools* (Plowden Report), London, HMSO, 1967.
37. See Chapter 8.
38. See Chapter 3.
39. *First Report of the Public Schools Commission*, Vol. 1, Note of Reservation to Chapter 10.
40. *Ibid.*, para. 478.
41. *Ibid.*, para. 366.
42. Additional terms of reference of the Public Schools Commission, page viii of both the First and the Second Reports of the commission.
43. *Second Report of the Public Schools Commission*, Vol. 1, para. 1.
44. *Ibid.*, para. 29.
45. *Ibid.*, para. 337.
46. Direct Grant Grammar Schools (Cessation of Grant) Regulations 1975, S.I. 1975/1198.
47. *Second Report of the Public Schools Commission*, Vol. 1, para. 54.
48. DES, *Education in Schools: A Consultative Document*, London, HMSO, 1977, Cmnd. 6869. See also C. B. Cox and R. Boyson (eds), *Black Paper 1977*, London, Temple Smith, 1977.
49. Education Act 1980, Sections 17 and 18.
50. Baroness Young. Debate on the assistance given by independent schools to state schools in Britain. House of Lords, 11 August 1984. Hansard, H. of L., p. 1204.
51. See Figure 1.

Chapter 2 (Councillors and Officers, pp. 21–36)

1. The two authorities were not alone in this practice. Saran's study of a local authority found that in the 1960s Labour and Conservative councillors alike accepted that the local education authority placed its brightest pupils in fee-paying schools (Saran 1973, p. 252).
2. A small number of 'middle schools deemed secondary' are included in this total. All figures are based on DES records for 1985.
3. Robart was one of the education authorities whose school governing bodies were studied by Kogan, Johnson and others in 1983 (see Kogan *et al.* 1984, p. 189)
4. Contraction of resources had prevented the computerisation task from progressing. The data were being used for manually produced forecasts for specific schools on an *ad hoc* basis rather than by computer for all schools.
5. An earlier attempt to establish the numbers of children in independent education in a more direct way, by asking the independent schools to supply this information directly to the county, had been abandoned. Many of the children on the rolls of local independent schools, especially

boarding schools, were not local in county terms (i.e. not resident in the county) and hence not relevant to the county's predictive estimates.
6. This view was not shared by all authorities. In 1984 Nottinghamshire attempted to exclude independent school pupils from access to certain authority-funded facilities such as music schools and swimming pools (see Ch. 11).
7. Wright Mills (1959, Ch. 1) discusses the distinction between the 'personal troubles of milieu and the public issues of social structure'. Patterns of administration in which places at fee-paying schools are individually funded as the response to personal difficulty tend to impede the recognition of educational coexistence as an enduring public issue.

Chapter 3 (Special Education and Boarding Education, pp. 37–48)

1. The Warnock Committee found that in 1977 there were 112 non-maintained special schools in England and Wales, of which 102 were residential. Their pupil populations constituted only 6 per cent of all full-time pupils in special schools, but included 82 per cent of all blind children and 45 per cent of all deaf children in special schools for the blind and deaf respectively. *Special Educational Needs*, Report of the Committee of Enquiry into the education of handicapped children and young people (Warnock Report), Cmnd. 7212, London, HMSO, 1978, para. 8.2.
2. 'Maladjustment' became an official category of handicap in 1945. Furlong (1985, pp. xi–xvi) discusses the history of the concept.
3. Department of Education and Science *Statistics of Education*, London, HMSO, 1979, Vol. 1, explanatory note 11.
4. Glennerster and Wilson (1970, p. 5) described the distinction between schools recognised as efficient and non-recognised schools as 'the major administrative division in the independent sector'. From 1961 to 1978 recognition as efficient was a positive requirement for any independent school providing special educational treatment for handicapped pupils. The recognition procedure ensured that HMI were an important reference group for these schools.
5. Section 7 of the Education Act 1981 sets out the duties of the local education authority in making and maintaining a statement of the special educational needs of a child who has been assessed as having such needs.
6. List supplied to the author by education department of Morrowshire.
7. Calculated as an average of four years (1979–82 inclusive).
8. The integration of children with special needs into mainstream schools is a continuing and controversial development with many specialist features which cannot be discussed here. Interest groups are, at the time of writing, arrayed on both sides of the argument.
9. Consideration for approval was only undertaken when the firm offer of a place was available from the school in question. This meant that the child must go for interview to a school which he or she might not, in the event,

be permitted to attend by the secretary of state, even though the school agreed to accept the child.

10. The DES limit for boarding pupils with special educational needs was fifty pupils per school. As a general rule, heads preferred not to have more than five pupils from any one authority, to limit the tendency for 'gangs' of pupils to be formed.

11. P. Coombes, a teacher at a dyslexic centre quoted by I. Smith, 'Pay Away', *Times Educational Supplement*, 15 March 1985.

12. The 1984/5 Annual Report of the Medical Research Council devoted three pages to a discussion of the research into 'deep' and 'surface' dyslexia being pursued at the Radcliffe Infirmary, Oxford, and of other research at University College, London, which had relevance for dyslexia. The MRC's *Handbook* for the same year listed two further projects with 'dyslexia' in the title.

13. Smith, *Times Educational Supplement*, 15 March 1985.

14. Education Act 1944, Section 61.

15. *Regina* v. *Hampshire County Council, ex parte* J. Queen's Bench Division, Mr Justice Taylor.

16. On the principle that continuity of education is desirable for the children of mobile parents, all ranks in all the armed services and members of the diplomatic service are eligible for boarding-school allowances for their children. The allowances are funded from the Defence Vote. The Services' boarding-school allowance, administered by the Service Children's Education Authority (SCEA) is not dependent on an overseas posting. SCEA provides a free advisory service to parents concerning boarding education for their children and liaises with both independent and maintained boarding schools. Expenditure on the Services boarding allowance was £71 million in 1984. The Foreign and Commonwealth Office does not provide an advisory or liaison service for diplomatic-service parents regarding their children's UK education. Choice of UK boarding schools is regarded as a personal matter for the family. In 1984 to 1985 the total cost of the diplomatic services boarding school allowance was £6.5 million. Less than 1 per cent of children receiving the allowance attended maintained boarding schools. Few such schools cater for junior-age children.

17. Martin Report, para. 10.

18. The Education (Miscellaneous Provisions) Act 1953, Section 6 (as amended by the Education Act 1981).

Chapter 4 (The Independent School, pp. 49–58)

1. The principal associations of which headteachers or schools may be in membership are: the Headmasters' Conference (HMC), the Incorporated Association of Preparatory Schools (IAPS), the Governing Bodies Association (GBA), the Girls' Schools Association (GSA), the Governing Bodies of Girls' Schools Association (GBGSA), the Society of Headmasters of Independent Schools (SHMIS) and the Independent Schools' Association Incorporated (ISAI). Other relevant organisations

are the Independent Schools Joint Council (ISJC), the Secondary Heads' Association (SHA) and the Independent Schools Information Service (ISIS).

2. Cadogan was not an IAPS school at the time of the research, but subsequently became one.

3. Headteachers or principals of maintained schools or colleges with pupils of post-compulsory school age were in a different position regarding the supply of pupils (see Ch. 5).

Chapter 5 (Supply of Pupils, pp. 59–70)

1. Problem pupils in maintained schools are, however, sometimes transferred to special units or tuition centres on a full- or part-time basis (see Bird *et al.* 1980, sect. 5.4).

2. The pamphlet *Independent Schools: The Facts* (ISIS, Doc. 12, 1982), claimed that small schools were the main reason given by parents contacting ISIS for choosing independent schools. The average size of an independent secondary school was 300 pupils, compared to an average size of over 800 in the maintained sector.

3. Exceptions to this general rule were the William Shakespeare School and Hilliers, both of which were for boys of secondary-school age only.

4. The question of post-compulsory pupil numbers is a separate issue, discussed in a later section of this chapter.

5. The letters were made available to the author, with the proviso that pupil names should not be disclosed.

6. Education Act 1980, Section 7.

7. Discussion in this section deals with 16-plus education, which is potentially within the range of secondary-school sixth forms. The whole question of what is now broadly known as 16–19 education in the maintained sector, an area of rapid proliferation of courses and institutional arrangements in the further-education field, cannot be covered here.

8. At two other colleges, research access was given to enrolment records. As a check against heads of departments' subjective impressions that between 10 and 20 per cent of full-time students on certain courses had previously been educated in the private sector, the records of 3,000 students were examined to establish where they had received their secondary education. For the years and the courses in question, the percentage of enrolled students who had previously attended private schools was for some courses substantially lower and for others substantially higher than the heads of departments had estimated. The exercise also demonstrated that identifying the status of a school (independent, maintained or voluntary aided) from its name and town of location is a painstaking and time-consuming task.

Chapter 6 (Managing Independent Schools, pp. 71–82)

1. Many children from ethnic-minority families, especially Asian families, are educated in independent schools, but teachers in independent schools do not appear to be gaining experience in explicitly multicultural education. A survey of HMC schools by Aston University found that most of the 42 per cent who replied saw no need for multicultural policies, although many of them had between 5 and 15 per cent of pupils from ethnic minorities (Cashmore and Bagley 1984).

2. For example, a letter to *The Guardian*, 24 September 1985, compared the pay of a teacher in an independent school unfavourably with that of a cleaner. Personal communications to the author also conveyed an impression of low pay to assistant teachers in independent schools.

3. As the dispute continued, protagonists expanded to include parents and all political parties in opposition, as well as central government, the employers, headteachers and the teachers themselves. Some observers suggested that things would never be the same again in maintained education (see, for example, Brighouse 1985).

4. In 1985 the major unions and the Professional Association of Teachers calculated the proportion of their members who taught in independent schools to be: AMMA, 15 per cent; NUT, 1.7 per cent; NAS/UWT, 1.5 per cent approx.; PAT, 2 per cent (including Scotland). These percentages accounted in total for approximately 17,000 teachers in independent schools, slightly over half of the full-time teachers listed in the ISIS census for 1985. It can be assumed that a substantial number of independent-school staff were not members of any union.

5. Education Act 1944, Section 61. As we saw in Chapter 3, this embargo is not always strictly observed.

6. For example, cases where tuition fees are paid by a local authority to enable a child to remain at an independent school following the death of a parent.

7. The Foundation School, like Hilliers, is a pseudonym for a famous public school. One of the families participating in the research had used the school (see Ch. 8).

8. The sum paid by a governor of the school which may be accompanied by the nomination of a particular pupil for admission to the school on means-tested fees.

9. As a rule a headteacher would have a say in any appointment of a bursar which occurred during the head's time at the school.

10. Our discussion of the respective responsibilities of headteachers and governors in independent schools is based on accounts given by headteachers. Guidelines for governors issued jointly by the GBA and GBGSA (1980) lay more emphasis on the overarching responsibilities of the governing body.

11. Most contemporary discussion of the relative merits of schools has centred around examination results. At their 1985 conference HMC were resisting pressure to publish exam results in a way which would enable the compiling of a league table. Bee and Dolton (1985) looked at

300 independent schools to see 'why their fees varied so much and whether they were delivering the expected exam success'. However, external examinations as a measure of value apply only to secondary schools. They are by no means all that parents weigh in the balance when evaluating schools.

12. Mrs Lennox, one of the parents interviewed, said, 'It is quite important to us that Broadacre has charitable status. We would certainly think twice about using any school which was run for profit.'

13. The brochure for Mallory House, a 'trust' school, pointed out that its charitable status meant it could not be maintained for private profit: 'It is very much to the schools' advantage that all its surplus revenue must be devoted to its improvement.'

14. The grounds on which schools have charitable status are explored by Salter and Tapper (1985, Ch. 4).

15. See, for example, the report by the National Confederation of Parent Teacher Associations, *The State of Schools in England and Wales*, Gravesend, NCPTA, 21 October 1985.

16. Reference to ISCO in the independent schools' brochures usually makes it clear that although the school supports the organisation through its membership, any call for individual advice is made at the expense of the parent.

Chapter 7 (Themes of Transfer to the Independent Sector, pp. 83–98)

1. For example Blyth (1967) and Davis (1950). More recently, Johnson and Ransom (1983) encouraged parents to evaluate their contribution to their children's education in their own terms rather than in response to a checklist devised by teachers.

2. Article 2 of the European Convention on Human Rights 'prohibits the state from preventing parents from arranging the education of their children outside the public school'. So long as the United Kingdom adheres to the convention, any attempt to abolish independent education would appear to be in breach of UK obligations.

3. The older daughters of the Morgan family may also come into this category. It was not clear whether the Catholic grammar school which two daughters attended during the 1960s was still a direct-grant school at that time. The school was outside the borders of the local education authority where the Morgans lived. The local authority met the cost of the secondary education of these two girls at the school and also of their younger sisters at the same school in the late 1960s and early 70s.

4. Glennerster and Wilson (1970, p. 71) estimate that the scheme reduced the fees of all fee-paying pupils by £70 per annum.

5. The question of various forms of help with fees which parents obtained is discussed in Chapter 9.

6. Parents interviewed by Fox believed that 'to remove the alternative provided by the private sector would both be a denial of the freedom that

is central to capitalism and succeed in finally removing the high academic standards that began with the disappearance of the grammar schools' (Fox 1984, p. 61). Nevertheless, only 18 per cent of Fox's parents explicitly referred to 'the lack of a grammar school in their area or the uncertainty that the boy would gain a place, as a factor in their decision' to use private education (Fox 1985, p. 136).

7. Mr Anthony defined his own direct-grant schooling as being in the state sector. This attitude, sincerely held by some individuals, that direct-grant schools were by no means in the private sector, meant that careful questioning was needed to establish an accurate picture of the parents' education.

8. Mrs Uden's comments included an appreciation of the teachers' grievance, but deplored their method of seeking its resolution. The reinforcement which this gave to her already unfavourable comparisons of the maintained with the private sector was a reaction anticipated by speakers at the Social Democratic Party's conference in 1985.

9. Mrs Ordwell's assessment of the 'maximising' effect of private pre-prep and preparatory schools was close to the *raison d'être* of Cadogan School (see Ch. 4), but this was not the school her sons attended.

10. Mrs Ordwell, during a childhood in a broken family, did in fact have a year or two of private boarding school while in the care of her father. But she had not taken her own education seriously until maturity.

11. This case is chiefly discussed in terms of the father's experience. Mr and Mrs Verrall had been married for over thirty years. They came from a similar background and shared the same educational values. In contrast to the many cases where the mother had been the prime mover in educational decisions, it was Mr Verrall who took responsibility for introducing his children to private education.

Chapter 8 (More Themes of Transfer, pp. 99–116)

1. Section 2 (8) of the Education Act 1980 states that a headteacher shall be a governor of the school by virtue of his office, 'unless he elects otherwise'.

2. Johnson and Ransom (1983) reported similar findings in their study of working-class families' relations with their children's schools.

3. The progressive or child-centred movement infiltrated gradually into education policy from 1914 onwards and received prominent support from the Plowden Report of 1966. Evetts (1974) contrasts the 'progressive ideal' with the 'knowledge ideal', which emphasises the need for subject-linked forms of understanding. Bennett (1976) discusses the progressive ideal in terms of its classroom application.

4. Another source of 'access' frustration for some parents was that the term when their children were eligible to enter primary school was linked with their month of birth. The fee-paying schools were more flexible, being willing to accept children with 'summer birthdays' at the beginning of the preceding school year.

5. The first statutory education appeals at local level were introduced into England and Wales in 1982. Stillman (1986) states that 10,000 cases were

heard in England alone by 1983. Replies to a questionnaire from the Information for Parental Choice (IPC) project indicated that 91 per cent of parents were offered a place at the school of their choice or the expected catchment area school. Between 1 and 1.5 per cent went to statutory appeal in 1984 but it appeared that 6 or 7 per cent of parents neither got the school they asked for nor went to statutory appeal. The questionnaire did not establish whether any of these parents turned to the private sector.

6. The IPC project found that although most parents were aware they could appeal against the allocation of a school place, not all distinguished clearly between the formal appeal procedure and the informal reviews with education officers which usually took place before appeals went forward (Stillman and Maychell 1986).

7. Only the Ordwells had done so.

8. Johnson and Ransom (1983) found that the smaller size and more intimate atmosphere of the primary school engendered strong emotions if antipathies arose between teacher and child, or between teacher and parent, at the primary stage.

9. 'Special agreement' voluntary schools were created by a once-for-all arrangement and are few in number (103 in 1980). The Education Act 1936 authorised authorities to pay specially favourable grants for the establishment of denominational secondary-modern schools and the Anglican and Roman Catholic churches were able to enter into special agreements with particular authorities for the furtherance of secondary reorganisation. Over 500 such agreements were entered into, but because of the war only thirty-seven materialised. The Education Act 1944 provided for the revival and implementation of any of the unfulfilled agreements on the original terms offered (Evans 1975, pp. 84, 99–100).

10. As already noted, Mrs Ewell was opposed to what she saw as the divisive tendencies of private education.

11. Communication to the author by the secretary of the society concerned, March 1985.

12. The experience was not cost-free to the family. All 'extras' were charged to them.

13. Lambert studied fifteen maintained boarding schools and fifty independent boarding schools of various kinds in the 1960s. See Lambert and Millham (1968) for an account of characteristics of these schools from the pupils' point of view.

14. Some authorities now refuse to grant boarding places to out-of-county children unless their home authority assumes responsibility for boarding as well as tuition costs since they have had experience of parents defaulting on their agreed contribution.

15. The Keegans had worked intensively for MENCAP. The Morgans, through their church, had played an important part in setting up local residential accommodation for handicapped young people.

16. With the implementation of the Education (Handicapped Children) Act 1970, all handicapped children, however serious their disability, became included in the framework of special education. Responsibility for these

children's education and training passed from the health authority to the local education authority.

17. This brief account does not do justice to the investment of energy, persistence and dedication which these parents had made in ensuring that their children gained access to suitable schools and centres. Those concerned with special education will know that such opportunities do not fall into the lap of parents.

Chapter 9 (Threshold of Affordability, pp. 117–129)

1. This reduction was, in effect, a 'grant from employer', but it was different in kind from benefits referred to under Column (f) of Figure 2, which were made by employers not themselves engaged in providing education.
2. Bursaries offered by the employer discussed here were available to children of either sex, from age 7 to 18, and there was no limitation to the number of children in one family who might benefit. Parents chose the schools and made arrangements for the child's education. The employer contacted the school with an enquiry about the potential of the child. It had been known for a bursary to be refused for the child of an eligible employee if an adverse report was received from the school on the child's potential and attitude.
3. In each case this particular kind of domino effect concerned two brothers.
4. Parents appeared hypersensitive to possible allegations of unfairness from their children. Similarity of education had not always been possible, especially in large families. Parents recalled spontaneously, sometimes twenty years after the event, whether those apparently disadvantaged had 'borne a grudge'.
5. In some cases the withdrawal of the child may be no reflection on the school but the outcome of a change of residence or other family circumstances. Similarly, the shareholder who sells out may do so to realise capital rather than as a response to the performance of the enterprise.
6. As already explained, this judgment sample was selected because the families exemplified differing patterns of use of the two sectors of education. Trends in the sample cannot therefore be extrapolated to a wider population of families.
7. Several parents used analogies with the National Health Service when discussing their children's state education. In the case of children who had had early health problems, mothers' battles with doctors sometimes seemed to have predisposed them to battle with teachers.

Chapter 10 (Two Systems or One? pp. 130–140)

1. See Note 50, Chapter 1.
2. Maintained schools were not openly in competition with the independent schools for financial support from parents, but it was claimed that

maintained education was becoming increasingly reliant on parental contributions towards essential education costs (NCPTA 1985).

3. The Education (Approval of Special Schools) Regulations, 1983, S.I. 1983, No. 1499. DES Circular 6/83 describes the effect of these regulations.

4. Robart education authority was in 1986 carrying out a consultative exercise with a view to absorbing more of these pupils into its own special schools.

5. See Note 15, Chapter 3.

6. Education Act 1980, Section 17 (1).

7. Section 17 (2) of the Act, on assisted places, refers to independent schools 'providing secondary education' and 'the desirability of securing an equitable distribution of assisted places throughout England and Wales and between boys and girls'.

8. *A Study of the Assisted Places Policy*, research directors G. Whitty and A. D. Edwards, SSRC 1982 (see Edwards *et al.* 1987, Fitz *et al.* 1987).

9. See, for example, Stevens (1980).

10. As already noted, parents in some areas are under pressure to make 'voluntary' contributions towards the costs of public sector schooling. The political principle involved is an important one, but the actual sums involved are minuscule compared with the commitment required from the family budget to pay for a place at an independent school.

11. Because of schools' individual admission policies, and the generally buoyant market for private education, getting a child into a school was never simply a question of writing a cheque. But parents did not feel as impotent or frustrated as when faced with procedures for choice in the maintained sector.

12. The words of Mrs Lennox, p. 104.

13. Mrs Quex described how the headteacher of Jeremy's maintained school sat back with a sigh of relief when she informed him that the boy, whom he recognised as able, was to be educated privately. His response appeared to be, 'Thank goodness that's one problem I haven't got to cope with any more.'

14. Seldon (1986) gives the chronology of various voucher proposals and responses to these.

15. Education Act 1980, Section 6 (3) (a).

16. See page 96.

Chapter 11 (Problems and Prospects, pp. 141–147)

1. Hilliers organised a week's 'incognito' exchange with the boy pupils of a co-educational comprehensive in a neighbouring authority. Visiting pupils were kitted out in the uniform of the famous school and mingled with its fee-paying pupils, while the boarders lived in the homes of the 'exchange' pupils and attended their comprehensive school for a week.

2. See Chapter 3.

3. In 1985 the General Synod of the Church of England agreed to consider

revising the composition and increasing the powers of the forty-three diocesan education committees. This would entail some loss of autonomy to the aided schools.

4. The Archbishop of Canterbury's Commission on Urban Priority Areas (1985) makes suggestions for change in church schools and for encouraging local participation in them. It does not suggest the church give up running the schools.

5. Some of the schools had been jointly founded, notably the Woodard schools. In the twentieth century the policy of the Woodard Corporation was to devolve as much autonomy as possible to individual schools (Gay 1985, p. 18).

6. The Archbishop's Commission on Urban priority (1985) found it a matter for regret that a number of clergy working in the inner city sent their children to private schools.

7. For example, the Christ-centred'schools whose curriculum is based on materials produced by Accelerated Christian Education of Louisville, Kentucky, USA.

8. For example, the Talmud Torah Machzikei Hadass School Trust, which in 1985 was the subject of a legal wrangle about its registration.

9. In some Bradford schools Halal meat is served, PE and swimming are done in single-sex groups, girls are allowed to wear trousers to school and track suits for PE, and rooms are set aside at lunch-times for prayers. See D. Lister, 'Muslims may soon get their own school', *Times Educational Supplement*, 30 August 1985.

10. *Ibid*.

11. Committee of Inquiry into the Education of Children from Ethnic Minority Groups. *Education for All* (Swann Report), London, HMSO, 1985.

12. See Figure 1, p. 7.

Education Tables

Table A Children's schooling in the public and private sectors of education

YEAR	19	52	53	54	55	56	57	58	59	60	61	62	63	64	65	66	67	68	69	70	71	72	73	74	75	76	77	78	79	80	81	82	83	84	85
Government		Conservative														Labour						Con.		/		Labour			/		Conservative				
Surname	Christian Name																																		
FELLOWES	Kim																																		
GRACEWELL	Rufus																																		
	Barnaby																																		
	Kevin																																		
	Dougal																																		
	Austin																																		
BARNETT	Colin																																		
	Mark																																		
	Julian																																		
	Benedict																																		
	Craig																																		
WINNICOTT	Sebastian																																		
	Oliver																																		
HENRY	Malcolm																																		
	Jessica																																		
	Rex																																		
ANTHONY	Nelson																																		
	Francesca																																		
CARDEW	Russell																																		
	Kathleen																																		
PEEL	Arnold																																		
	Camilla																																		
	Preston																																		
DARE	Melanie																																		
	Nathan																																		
KEEGAN	Desmond																																		
	Deborah																																		
	Charlotte																																		
MORGAN	Ruth																																		
	Cecilia																																		
	Edward																																		
	Martha																																		
	Bernadette																																		
	Naomi																																		
	Philip																																		
	Stephen																																		
JOSS	Noel																																		
	Piers																																		
EWELL	Jason																																		
	Bridget																																		

The chart shows education histories plotted against governments over time. Columns are grouped under governments: Conservative / Labour / Con. / Labour / Conservative.

Surname	Christian Name	Conservative	Labour	Con.	Labour	Conservative
ORDWELL	Carl		********xxxxxxxxxxxxx	££££££££££££££	xxxxxxxxxxxxxxxxxxxxxxxxxxxx	
	Donald				********££££££££££££££££££££	
	Murray					********££££££££££££
SLIEMAN	Reah	****xxxxxxxxxxxxxxxxxxxxxxxxxxxx				
	Darrell		****xxxxxxxxxxxxxxxxxxxxxxxxx	££££££££££££££££££££££££		
ZARO	Damien			********xxxxxxxxxxxxxx	££££££££££££££££££	
	Nancy				************xxxxxxxxxxxxxxxx	xxx
	Dudley					Born
NORLAND	Peregrine	********xxxxxxxxxxxxxxxxx	££££££££££££££££££££££££££££££££££			
	Laura		********xxxxxxxxxxx	££££££££££££££££££££		
	Rebecca		********xxxxxxxxxxxxxx	xxxxxxxxxxxxxxxxxxxxxxxxxxxxxxxxxxxxxxxxxxx		
	Denzil					********££££££££££££££
YALT	Deidre	********xxxxxxxxxxxxxxx	££££££££££££££££££	xxxxxxxx		
	Ian		********££			
IRWIN	Norman	xxxxxxxxxxxxxxxxxxxxxxxxxxxxxxxxxxxxxxxxxxx				
	Judith	xxxxxxxxxxxxxxxxxxxxxxxxx££££££££££££££££££££££				
	Glenda	***xxxxxxxxxxx££££££££xxxx££££££££££££££££££££xxxxxxxxx				
	Penelope	xxxxxxxxxxx££££££££££££££xxxxxxxxxxxxxxxxxxxxx				
	Adrian		********xxxxxxxxxxxxxxx££££££££££££££££££££££££			££££££££££
ROLAND	Max		****xxxxxxxxxxxxxxxxx££££££££££££££££££££££££			
	Alison		****xxxxxxxxxxxxxxxxxxxxxxxxxxxxxxxxxxxx			
QUEX	Jeremy					********xxxxxxxxxxx££££££££££
	Brian					********xxxxxxxxx££££££££
LENNOX	Alexander			********xxxxxxxx	££££££££££	
	Claudia					********xxxxxxx££££££££££
TANNER	Ralph					********xxxxxxx££££££££££
	Caroline					********££xxxxxxxxx
	Alan					********
VERRALL	Jennifer	xxxxxxxxxxxxxxxxxxxxxx££££££££££££££££££££££££££££££				
	Charlton	xxxxxxxxx££££££££££££££££££££££££££££££££££££				
	Raymond		xxxxxxxx££££££££££££££££££££££££££££££££££££££			
	Josephine		xxxxxxxxxxxxxxxxxxxxxxxxxxxxxxxxxx			
UDEN	Rodney			********££££££££££££££	xxxxxxxxxxxxxxxxxx	
	Dennis					********££££££££££££££££££

Key:

*********	Pre-school
xxxxxxxx	Maintained school
££££££££	Fee-paying school

167

Table B

YEAR			1923	24	25	26	27	28	29	30	31	32	33	34	35	36	37	38	39	40	41
Government			Con	/ Lab /		Conservative		/	Labour	/		Coalition	/	Con	/		Coalition		/		
No.	Name	W (ife) / H (usband)																			
1	Fellowes	W / H																ooooooo	oooooooo		
2	Gracewell	W / H								ooooooooooooooooooooooo				ØØØØØØØØØØØ	ØØØØØ		ooooooo	ooooooo	oooooooo	oooooooo		
3	Barnett	W / H					ooooooooooooooooooooo				ØØØØØØØØØØØØØØØ	ØØØØ									
4	Winnicott	W / H																	oooooooo	oooo		
5	Henry	W / H																				
6	Anthony	W / H																				
7	Cardew	W / H		ooooooooooooooooooooooo					ØØØØØØØØØØØØØØ					ooooooo	ooooooo	oooooooo	oooooooo	oooooooo	ØØ			
8	Peel	W / H														ooooooo	ooooooo	oooooooo	oooo		oooo	
9	Dare	W / H								ooooooooooooooooo							ØØØØØØØ			oooo	
10	Keegan	W / H																				
11	Morgan	W / H							oooooooooooooooooooo				ØØØØØØØØØØØØØØØ	ØØØØ							
12	Joss	W / H																				
13	Ewell	W / H												ooooooooooooooooo		ØØØØØ		ooooooo	oooooooo			
14	Ordwell	W / H																				
15	Slieman	W / H											ooooooooooooooo		ØØØØØ		oooooooo	oooooooo			
16	Zaro	W / H																				
17	Norland	W / H																				
18	Yalt	W / H																ooooooo	oooooooo			
19	Irwin	W / H							ooooooooooooooooo			ØØØØØØØØØ		oooooooo	oooooooo	oooooooo					
20	Roland	W / H													ooooooo	ooooooo	oooooooo	oooooooo	ØØ			
21	Quex	W / H																			oooo	
22	Lennox	W / H																				
23	Tanner	W / H																				
24	Verrall	W / H																ooooooo	oooooooo	oooooooo		
25	Uden	W																				

Note: This table shows the period during which each parent was at school. It does not indicate whether their education was in the public or private sector, nor whether their education after age 11 was at an elementary or secondary school.

Parents' years at school

42	43	44	45	46	47	48	49	50	51	52	53	54	55	56	57	58	59	60	61	62	63	64	65	66	67	68

National (WAR) /   Labour   /   Conservative   /   Labour

Key: ooo = aged 5 to 10 plus

          ØØØ = aged 11 and over

References and Bibliography

Adelman, C. *et al*. (1984). Rethinking case study, in J. Bell *et al*. (eds.), *Conducting Small-scale Investigations in Educational Management*, London, Harper and Row.

Archbishop of Canterbury's Commission on Urban Priority Areas (1985). *Faith in the City*. London, Church House Publishing Co.

Bauer, P. T. (1978). *Class on the Brain*. London, Centre for Policy Studies.

Beales, A. C. F. (1970). *Education: a Framework for Choice*. London, Institute of Economic Affairs.

Beattie, N. (1985). *Professional Parents*. London, Falmer Press.

Bee, M. and Dolton, P. J. (1985). Costs and economies of scale in U.K. private schools. *Applied Economics*, 17(2), 281–90.

Beer, S. H. (1982). *Britain Against Itself*. London, Faber and Faber.

Bennett, N. (1976). *Teaching Styles and Pupil Progress*. London, Open Books.

Bird, C. *et al*. (1980). *Disaffected Pupils*. Uxbridge, Brunel University.

Blyth, W. (1967). Some relationships between homes and schools, in M. Craft *et al*., (eds.), *Linking Home and School*, London, Longman.

Board of Education (1943). *Educational Reconstruction*. Cmnd. 6458. London, HMSO.

(1944). *Report of the Committee on Public Schools* (Fleming Report). London, HMSO.

Borcherding, T. E. (ed.) (1977). *Budgets and Bureaucrats: The Sources of Government Growth*. Durham, NC, Duke University Press.

Brighouse, T. (1985). Who will be left when the pay dispute ends? London, *Times Educational Supplement*, 22 November.

Burgess, R. G. (ed.) (1982). *Field Research: A Sourcebook and Field Manual*. London, Allen and Unwin.

(ed.) (1984). *The Research Process in Educational Settings: Ten Case Studies*. London, Falmer Press.

Burnett, J. (1982). *Destiny Obscure*. London, Allen Lane.

Cashmore, E. and Bagley, C. (1984). Colour blind. *Times Educational Supplement*, London, 12 August.

Central Advisory Council for Education, England (1967). *Children and their Primary Schools* (Plowden Report). London, HMSO.

Checkland, S. (1983). *British Public Policy, 1776–1939*. Cambridge, Cambridge University Press.

Committee of Inquiry into the Education of Children from Ethnic Minority Groups (1985). *Education for All* (Swann Report). London, HMSO.

Conservative Political Centre (1985). No turning back. London, CPC.

Cox, C. B. and Boyson, R. (eds.) (1977). *Black Paper 1977*. London, Temple Smith.

Croall, J. (1987). *Don't You Know There's a War On? Women, Children and Outsiders, 1939–45*. London, Deutsch.

Crosland, C. A. R. (1964). *The Future of Socialism*. London, Jonathan Cape.

Davis, A. (1950). *Social Class Influence on Learning*. Chicago, University of Chicago Press.

Dennison, S. R. (1984). *Choice in Education*. London, Institute of Economic Affairs.

Dent, H. C. (1968). *The Education Act, 1944*. London, University of London Press.

Department of Education and Science (1977). *Education in Schools*. A Consultative Document. Cmnd. 6869. London, HMSO.

(1978). *Special Educational Needs: Report of the Committee of Enquiry into the Education of Handicapped Children and Young People* (Warnock Report). Cmnd. 7212. London, HMSO.

(1985). *Better Schools*. Cmnd. 9469. London, HMSO.

Devlin. T. (1984). *Choosing Your Independent School*. London, ISIS and Arrow Books.

Dexter, L. A. (1970). *Elite and Specialised Interviewing*. Evanston, IL, Northwestern University Press.

Edwards, A. D., Fitz, J. and Whitty, G. (1987). *Plucking Embers from the Ashes? A Study of the Origins, Implementation and Consequences of the Assisted Places Scheme*. Lewes, Falmer Press.

Evans, K. (1975). *The Development and Structure of the English Educational System*. London, Hodder and Stoughton.

Evetts, J. (1974). *The Sociology of Educational Ideas*. London, Routledge and Kegan Paul.

Finch, J. (1984) *Education as Social Policy*. London, Longman.

Fitz, J., Edwards, A. D. and Whitty, G. (1987). *Beneficiaries, Benefits and Costs: An investigation of the Assisted Places Scheme*. Research Papers in Education. Slough, NFER.

Flew, A. (1983). *Power to the People!* London, Centre for Policy Studies.

Floud, J. *et al.* (1956). *Social Class and Educational Opportunity*. London, Heinemann.

Fox, I. (1984). The demand for a public school education: a crisis of confidence in comprehensive schooling, in G. Walford (ed.), *British Public Schools: Policy and Practice*, London, Falmer Press.

Fox, I. (1985). *Private Schools and Public Issues*. London, Macmillan.

Fraser, E. (1959). *Home Environment and the School*. London, University of London Press.

Friedman, M. (1962). *Capitalism and Freedom*. Chicago, University of Chicago Press.

Furlong, V. J. (1985). *The Deviant Pupil: Sociological Perspectives*. Milton Keynes, Open University Press.

Gay, B. M. (1985). *The Church of England and the Independent Schools*. Abingdon, Culham Educational Foundation.

Glennerster, H. (ed.) (1983). *The Future of the Welfare State*. London, Heinemann.

Glennerster, H. and Wilson, G. (1970). *Paying for Private Schools*. London, Allen Lane.

Gosden, P. H. J. H. (1976). *Education in the Second World War*. London, Methuen.

(1983) *The Education System Since 1944*. Oxford, Martin Robertson.

GBA and GBGSA (1980). *Guidelines for Governors*, Petersfield, Document 208, January.

Griggs, C. (1985). *Private Education in Britain*. London, Falmer Press.

Halsey, A. H. *et al.* (1980). *Origins and Destinations*. Oxford, Clarendon Press.

Hill, M. (1983). *Understanding Social Policy*. 2nd edn. Oxford, Basil Blackwell and Martin Robertson.

Hirschman, A. O. (1970). *Exit, Voice and Loyalty*. Cambridge, Mass., Harvard University Press.

Honey, J. F. de S. (1977). *Tom Brown's Universe*. London, Millington. ISIS (1982). *Independent Schools: The Facts*.

ISIS Document 12 (rev. March 1982).

Itzin, C. (1985). *How to Choose a School*. London, Methuen.

Jackson, B. and Marsden, D. (1963). *Education and the Working Class*. London, Routledge and Kegan Paul.

Jackson, C. (1985). *Who Will Take Our Children?* London, Methuen.

Johnson, D. (1982). Research into home school relations, 1970–80, in L. Cohen *et al.* (eds.), *Educational Research and Development in Britain 1970–1980*, Windsor, NFER-Nelson.

Johnson, D. and Ransom, E. (1983). *Family and School*. London, Croom Helm.

Jowell, R. and Airey, C. (eds.) (1984). *British Social Attitudes*. Aldershot, Gower.

Kogan, M. (1978). *The Politics of Educational Change*. London, Fontana.

(1983). The central–local government relationship: a comparison between the education and health services. *Local Government Studies*, 9 (1), Jan./Feb., 65–85.

Kogan, M. *et al.* (1984). *School Governing Bodies*. London, Heinemann Educational Books.

Lambert, R. (1966). *The State and Boarding Education*. London, Methuen.

(1975). *The Chance of a Lifetime?* London, Weidenfeld and Nicolson.

Lambert, R. and Millham, S. (1968). *The Hothouse Society: An Exploration of*

Boarding School Life through the Boys' and Girls' Own Writings. London, Weidenfeld and Nicolson.

Leinster-Mackay, D. (1984). *The Rise of the English Prep School*. London, Falmer Press.

Lister, D. (1985). Muslims may soon get their own school. *Times Educational Supplement*, London, 30 August.

Miles, M. N. and Huberman, A. M. (1984). *Qualitative Data Analysis: A Sourcebook of New Methods*. Beverly Hills, Sage.

Ministry of Education. (1960). *Report of the Working Party on Assistance with the Cost of Boarding Education* (Martin Report). London, HMSO.

National Confederation of Parent Teacher Associations (1985). *The State of Schools in England and Wales: A Report*. Gravesend, NCPTA, 21 October.

Nisbet, J. and Watt, J. (1980). *Case Study*. Rediguide 26: Guides in Educational Research. Nottingham, University of Nottingham, School of Education.

Parkinson, M. (1970). *The Labour Party and the Organisation of Secondary Education, 1918–65*. London, Routledge and Kegan Paul.

Pinker, R. (1971). *Social Theory and Social Policy*. London, Heinemann Educational Books.

Public Schools Commission (1968). *First Report of the Public Schools Commission*. Vol. 1, *Report*. Vol. 2, *Appendices*. London, HMSO.

(1970). *Second Report of the Public Schools Commission*. Vol. 1, *Report on Independent Day Schools and Direct Grant Grammar Schools*. Vol. 2, *Scotland*. Vol. 3, *Appendices*. London, HMSO.

Ranson, S. *et al.* (eds.) (1985). *Between Centre and Locality*. London, Allen and Unwin.

Rhodes, R. A. W. (1977). *Central–local relations in Britain: A Review of the Literature and a Framework for Analysis*. London SSRC.

Salter, B. and Tapper, T. (1985). *Power and Policy in Education: The Case of Independent Schooling*. London, Falmer Press.

Sampson, A. (1982). *The Changing Anatomy of Britain*. London, Hodder and Stoughton.

Saran, R. (1973). *Policy-making in Secondary Education: A Case Study*. Oxford, Clarendon Press.

Seldon, A. (1986). *The Riddle of the Voucher*. London, Institute of Economic Affairs.

Shaw, B. (1983). *Comprehensive Schooling: The Impossible Dream?* Oxford, Basil Blackwell.

Silvey, J. (1975). *Deciphering Data*. London, Longman.

Smith, B. L. R. (ed.) (1975). *The New Political Economy: The Public Use of the Private Sector*. London, Macmillan.

Smith, I. (1985). Pay Away. *Times Educational Supplement*, London, 15 March.

Social Democratic Party (1983). *Education and Training*. Policy Document No. 6. London, SDP.

Socialist Educational Association (1981). *The Dual System of Voluntary and County Schools*. Discussion Document. Manchester, SEA.

Socialist Educational Association (1986). *All Faiths in All Schools: Second Report of the S.E.A. on Voluntary Schools and Religious Education*. Draft Discussion Document. London, SEA.

Social Science Research Council (1979). *Central–Local Government Relations: A Panel Report to the Research Initiatives Board*. Appendix. London, SSRC.

Stevens, A. (1980). *Clever Children in Comprehensive Schools*. Harmondsworth, Penguin.

Stewart, J. (1983). *Local Government: The Conditions of Local Choice*. London, Allen and Unwin.

Stillman, A. (1986). Maintaining the Balance with the Statutory Appeal, in A. Stillman (ed.), *The Balancing Act of 1980: Parents, Politics and Education*, Slough, NFER.

Stillman, A. and Maychell, K. (1986). *Choosing Schools: Parents, LEAs and the 1980 Education Act*. Windsor, NFER–Nelson.

Tawney, R. H. (1931). *Equality*. London, Allen and Unwin, 1964.

Taylor, G. and Saunders, J. B. (1976). *The Law of Education*. 8th edn. London, Butterworths.

Walford, G. (ed.) (1984). *British Public Schools: Policy and Practice*. London, Falmer Press.

Welton, J. *et al.* (1982). *Meeting Special Educational Needs: The 1981 Act and Its Implications*. Bedford Way Papers 12. Institute of Education, London University.

West, E. G. (1970). *Education and the State*. 2nd edn. London, Institute of Economic Affairs.

(1975). *Education and the Industrial Revolution*. London, Batsford.

Wright Mills, C. (1959). *The Sociological Imagination*. New York, Oxford University Press.

Yin, R. K. (1984). *Case Study Research: Design and Methods*. Beverly Hills, Sage.

Index